1st American ed. 15ª

WODEHOUSE AT WAR

WODEHOUSE
AT WAR

IAIN SPROAT

New Haven and New York
TICKNOR & FIELDS
1981

CONTENTS

ACKNOWLEDGEMENTS

I should like to acknowledge with gratitude the help I have received from the following: the Home Office, London; the Foreign and Commonwealth Office, London; the Ministry of Defence, London; the Embassy of the Federal German Republic, London; the Foreign Office of the Federal German Republic, Bonn; the Bundesarchiv, Koblenz; the Embassy of Sweden, London; the Embassy of Switzerland, London; the Swiss Foreign Office, Berne; the Embassy of the United States of America, London; the Columbia Broadcasting System; the Milo Ryan Phonoarchive, the University of Washington, Seattle; the U.S. Army Military History Institute; National Archives and Records, Washington D.C.: the British Broadcasting Corporation; the Public Records Office; the Library of the House of Commons; the Professional Golfers' Association; the British Library; the Commonwealth War Graves Commission; Mrs. Thelma Cazalet-Keir; Mr. Joseph Connelly; Mr. David Jasen; Mrs. Rosemary Drake; Mr. Christopher Maclehose; Mr. Nigel Nicolson; Lord Norwich; and Frau Elisabeth Schäffer.

I should like particularly to express my great thanks to two other persons. First, Mrs. Jacqueline Powell (formerly Miss Jacqueline Grant) for all her help and advice, and for making available to me various of her family papers. Second, Herr Werner Plack, who gave me so much of his time, and answered so courteously so many points from his unrivalled knowledge of the tangled events surrounding P. G. Wodehouse in Germany and France from 1940 to 1944.

I should also like to thank Mrs. Sheena Reid for so efficiently typing the manuscript of this book.

By the year of his death in 1975, at the age of 93, Pelham Grenville Wodehouse had won great literary honours and success. He had been knighted by Queen Elizabeth II. He had been made a Doctor of Letters by the University of Oxford. Books had been written devoted to critical analysis of his work. A collection of essays, entitled "Homage to P. G. Wodehouse", had been published in his honour. He was acknowledged, as widely and as surely as it is possible for such things to be acknowledged during a man's lifetime, to be a writer of genius.

Furthermore, unlike many writers of genius, P. G. Wodehouse was commercially successful. He became a very rich man. His industry was prodigious: it encompassed books, plays, musical comedies and films.

Wodehouse wrote 98 books. His first novel, "The Pothunters", was published in 1902, and he was working on his last, "Sunset at Blandings" – published posthumously and unfinished – shortly before his death in 1975. Over these 73 years, sales of Wodehouse's books ran into many millions, and for each book sold he would receive a royalty, rarely less than ten per cent of the retail price, and frequently more. For example, by the date of Wodehouse's death, the sales of one of his novels alone. "Thank You, Jeeves", numbered some three million copies.

Nor were royalties the only source of revenue from his books: there were also fees from magazines, for the serialisation of novels, and for the publication of short stories in the magazines before being collected in book form. These fees could be substantial. In 1932, Cosmopolitan paid Wodehouse what was his highest serialisation fee of $50,000 for "Thank You, Jeeves". For reasons of their own, Cosmopolitan did not actually publish "Thank You, Jeeves" until December 1933 – by which time the Saturday Evening Post was also serialising another Wodehouse novel, "Right-ho Jeeves", which it had bought from Wodehouse for $40,000.

In addition to his 98 books, Wodehouse also had a hand in some

50 plays and musical comedies, either as author, translator or lyric writer. He wrote lyrics for over 200 songs. In 1917, no less than five musical comedies to which he had contributed were running simultaneously on Broadway, New York – a record never surpassed. In 1935 he wrote to his old school friend and fellow author, Bill Townend: "Just got the 'Anything Goes' script from America. There are two lines of mine left in it, and so far I am receiving £50 a week apiece for them. That's about £3.10.0 a word which is pretty good payment, though less, of course, than my stuff is worth."

He was also involved – with varying degrees of involvement – in writing the scripts of 25 films. In 1930, for example, he was paid $2,000 a week for a year to work on film scripts in Hollywood. In 1936 he worked in Hollywood for six months at $2,500 a week. What is more, on both occasions, the film studio gave him so little work to do that he had plenty of free time to devote to his own novels and short stories – which enabled him to earn even more money from the same work-time.

But honour and money were not the end of Wodehouse's good fortune: he was also very happily married for over 60 years. On 30th September 1914, in New York, Wodehouse married Ethel May Rowley. She had been born Ethel Newton, on 23rd May 1885, at King's Lynn, Norfolk, England. She was the widow of a British engineer, Joseph Arthur Leonard Rowley, who had died in 1908, after only five years of marriage, from drinking infected water in India. By her first marriage, she had a daughter, Leonora, to whom Wodehouse was deeply attached, and whom he legally adopted.

In character, Wodehouse was kind, generous, straightforward, hard-working, modest, quiet, and steady. His humour was never malicious. He never displayed the volatility of temperament or egocentricity of so many creative geniuses. He showed fortitude when doctors informed him – wrongly, as it turned out – that he had a brain tumour, and, later, that he was going blind; this fortitude and steady spirit he also showed, as described later in this book, while interned in various German camps during the Second World War.

Wodehouse was a genuinely good man.

Yet, in spite of his worldly success, his domestic happiness, and his steady character, over his name and honour for the last 35 years of his life there hung a dark shadow which even the award of a knighthood in January 1975 did not wholly dispel.

This shadow was the result of what was believed to be Wodehouse's behaviour following his arrest by the Nazis in France in May 1940.

There were two reasons why Wodehouse's reputation remained so tragically tarnished by these events from 1941 until the day of his death. The first was that he himself never gave any full account of them. The reasons for this are given later in this book. The second is that, for 35 years, the British Government refused to make public the evidence and conclusions of the investigation into Wodehouse's wartime activities which was conducted by Major E. J. P. Cussen of the Intelligence Corps (later a judge) on behalf of the British security service, M.I.5, in 1944 and 1945. This evidence was kept secret until 1980 when, after repeated, but rejected, requests by myself to successive British Governments, I was eventually granted permission to examine it. The reasons why this evidence was kept secret for so long are discussed later in this book.

✽　✽　✽

The substance of the charges against Wodehouse which led to him being branded as a coward and a traitor may be summarised as follows: that, living in France in 1940, he made no attempt to escape from the advancing German Army; that he and his wife willingly entertained Germans in their house at Le Touquet, and later in various hotels and private houses in Germany and France; that he was a Nazi sympathiser; that during the internment by the Germans he was granted special privileges as a reward for collaborating with the Germans; that he was specially released by the Germans in 1941 on condition that he would broadcast pro-Nazi propaganda from Berlin; that, like William Joyce, nick-named "Lord Haw-Haw", who was executed for treason after the war, Wodehouse did in fact broadcast such propaganda; and that he thereafter lived a life of contemptible ease and luxury in Berlin and Paris for the rest of the war, paid for by the Germans as a reward for his help for their war effort.

✽　✽　✽

In outline, the chronology of Wodehouse's wartime activities was as follows: in 1939, on the outbreak of war, Plum (the name by which he was always known to his family and friends) and Ethel Wodehouse were living in a house called Low Wood, at Le Touquet in France. They had first come to live at Le Touquet in June 1934, and, apart from a year's visit to the United States from November 1936 until November 1937, and shorter visits to the United Kingdom, had lived there until 1940. On 22nd May 1940, the Germans occupied Le Touquet, and thereafter Wodehouse was required to report at nine o'clock each morning to the German authorities in the nearby town of Paris Plage. On 26th May 1940, the evacuation of Dunkirk began. On 22nd June peace terms were signed between France and Germany. On 21st July Wodehouse was told that, together with twelve other male aliens in Le Touquet, he was to be committed to an internment camp. That day, he was driven by bus to the prison at Loos, a suburb of Lille, about 70 miles from Le Touquet. The journey took seven hours, the bus stopping on several occasions to pick up other male aliens.

Within a week, all those who were aged over 60 were released under the terms of a Regulation to that effect issued by the German Ministry of the Interior on 5th September 1939, and not rescinded until late in 1942 – then at the urging of the Gestapo. Those internees then remaining, including Wodehouse and numbering 44, were taken to a nearby railway station where they met 800 other male internees and all of them were transported by cattle trucks, 50 men to a truck, to Liége in Belgium. This rail journey took nineteen hours. They were then imprisoned in the former Belgian Army barracks at Liége. Here they remained for a week.

On 3rd August 1940, all the internees, including Wodehouse, were again packed into cattle trucks and arrived at Huy, after a journey of six hours. Here they were imprisoned in the medieval stone fortress, called the Citadel.

Wodehouse and the other internees remained at the Citadel of Huy, under primitive conditions – Wodehouse slept on thin straw on a stone floor – and on meagre rations, for some six weeks. On 8th September 1940, the internees were taken to a railway station, put into regular passenger compartments, eight men to a compartment. Each man was given one sausage and half a loaf; 32 hours later, they were given another half loaf and some soup. This was their only food on a journey that lasted three days and nights. Their destination was a former lunatic asylum in the village of Tost, in Upper Silesia, then in Germany; after the end of the war in 1945, in Poland. Wodehouse remained an internee at Tost until he was released on 21st June 1941, and taken to Berlin.

During the following four weeks, Wodehouse made five broadcasts from Berlin on German radio. The exact dates on which Wodehouse recorded the talks, as opposed to the dates on which the Germans broadcast them, cannot now be precisely established, but the first was recorded on 25th June and the last on 26th July.

The actual transmission of the five talks was as follows: the first talk was broadcast to the United States on 28th June 1941. The second on 9th July. The third on 23rd July. The fourth on 30th July. The fifth on 6th August. In addition, the five talks were separately broadcast by the Germans to the United Kingdom on, respectively, 9th, 10th, 11th, 12th and 14th August 1941.

In addition to the talks on German radio, Wodehouse also took part in a short interview in Berlin with the Columbia Broadcasting System's correspondent, Harry W. Flannery, on 26th June 1941. (The United States was still neutral at this date.) This interview, and its unhappy consequences, are described in detail later in this book.

Continuing the chronology of Wodehouse's war-time activities, after he was released from Tost he remained in Berlin from 22nd June until 27th June. He then departed to the house of the fiancée of an old Hollywood friend, Baron Raven von Barnikow, at Degenershausen in the Harz mountains. Details of this arrangement are given later in this book. Twice Wodehouse travelled from this house to Berlin, a journey of some five hours, to record the later talks. After his wife arrived in Berlin on 27th July 1941, from Hesdin in France where she had been staying, both the Wodehouses stayed at Degenershausen until the end of November 1941, when they were forced to return to Berlin because there was no heating in the house. They both stayed at the Adlon Hotel in Berlin until April 1942, when Wodehouse returned to Degenershausen. His wife remained in Berlin. In November 1942 Wodehouse returned to Berlin, and again stayed at the Adlon Hotel, except for one month which they spent at the Bristol Hotel. In April 1943 both the Wodehouses went to stay as paying guests of Count and Countess Wolkenstein at Lobnis in

11

Upper Silesia. The Wolkensteins were friends of a Frau von Wulfing, an English woman married to a German and living in Berlin.

On 9th September 1943 the Wodehouses were allowed to leave for France, where they stayed at the Hotel Bristol in Paris. They remained there until the Allies liberated Paris on 25th August 1944.

The enquiry conducted by Major Cussen on behalf of M.I.5, into Wodehouse's behaviour, was completed on 28th September 1944. It is important for the reader to note how early is this last date: only a month and three days after the Allies reached Paris. In September 1944, with the war still in progress, it was not possible for Cussen to see all the relevant evidence, such as records in German possession, or to question all the relevant individuals, such as Wodehouse's fellow internees. Cussen's investigation, although the greatest single contribution towards proving Wodehouse's innocence, does not, of itself, prove it. Certainly, and most importantly, it found no acceptable evidence of Wodehouse's guilt. But, of necessity, because of the early date at which Cussen's investigation was undertaken, it could not positively prove his innocence. Cussen's report is seriously wrong in some places, and misleading in others, as will be shown by other evidence set out later in this book.

*　　*　　*

The public reputation of those in war-time Britain who, following Wodehouse's release and broadcasts, made the charges of collaboration and treason against him, was such as to lend overwhelming weight to them.

The B.B.C. – whose war-time reputation for broadcasting the truth was unsurpassed – urged on by the Minister of Information in Churchill's war-time Government, Duff Cooper, appeared to pour upon Wodehouse, in one broadcast, on 15th July 1941, what was probably the most vituperative vilification ever poured on one man. The author of this broadcast was William Connor, then the columnist "Cassandra" of the Daily Mirror. The ferocity of his attack on Wodehouse can be judged by the following passage from it: "I have come to tell you tonight of the story of a rich man trying to make his last and greatest sale – that of his own country. It is a sombre story of honour pawned to the Nazis for the price of a soft bed in a luxury hotel. It is the record of P. G. Wodehouse ending forty years of money-making fun with the worst joke he ever made in his life. The only wisecrack he ever pulled that the world received in silence.

"When the war broke out, Pelham Grenville Wodehouse was at Le Touquet – gambling. Nine months later he was still there. Poland had been wiped out. Denmark had been overrun and Norway had been occupied. Wodehouse still went on with his fun. The elderly playboy didn't believe in politics. He said so. No good-time Charlie ever does. Wodehouse was throwing a cocktail party when the storm-troopers clumped in on his shallow life. They led him away – the funny Englishman with his vast repertoire of droll butlers, amusing young men and comic titled fops. Politics, in the form of the Nazi Eagle, came home to roost. Bertie Wooster faded and Dr. Goebbels hobbled on the scene. . . .

"He treated his prisoner gently. Wodehouse was stealthily groomed for stardom, the most disreputable stardom in the world – the limelight of Quislings. On the last day of June of this year, Dr. Goebbels was ready. So too was Pelham Wodehouse. He was eager and he was willing, and when they offered him Liberty in a country that has killed Liberty, he leapt at it.

"And Dr. Goebbels taking him into a high mountain, showed unto him all the Kingdoms of the world . . . and said unto him: 'All this power will I give thee if thou wilt worship the Führer.'

"Pelham Wodehouse fell on his knees.

"Perhaps you have heard this man's voice reaching out to you from his luxury suite on the third floor of the Adlon Hotel in Berlin. Maybe you can forgive him.

"Some of us can neither forgive nor forget.

"Fifty thousand of our countrymen are enslaved in Germany. How many of them are in the Adlon Hotel tonight?

"Barbed wire is their pillow.

"They endure – but they do not give in.

"They suffer – but they do not sell out.

"Between the terrible choice of betrayal of one's country and the abominations of the Gestapo, they have only one answer.

"The gaols of Germany are crammed with men who have chosen without demur. But they have something that Wodehouse can never regain. Something that thirty pieces of silver could never buy . . .''

Wodehouse was denounced, too, in Parliament: on 9th July 1941, the then Foreign Secretary, Anthony Eden (later Lord Avon) accused him of having "lent his services to the Nazi war propaganda machine". Quintin Hogg, M.P. (later Lord Hailsham) called him a traitor and compared him to "Lord Haw-Haw," saying, " . . .while he was clowning, British boys were resisting the Germans, and there can be nothing but contempt for the action of a man who, in order to live in a hotel more comfortably than his fellow-prisoners, did that kind of thing against his country . . ."

The flavour of much contemporary feeling in the United Kingdom about Wodehouse's broadcasts from Berlin, can be judged from the letters about them which appeared in those two leading national newspapers, the Daily Telegraph and The Times in July 1941, following the first of the broadcasts. Of those who wrote to the Daily Telegraph, whose names were well known to the contemporary public, Ian Hay (pseudonym of Major-General John Hay Beith, M.C.), was a best-selling author, mainly of light romances, excellent of their kind, such as "Pip"; he was also author of a once famous and moving account of the first months of the First World War, "The First Hundred Thousand". From 1938 to 1941, Hay was Director of Public Relations at the War Office; he was a good friend of Wodehouse, and had collaborated with him on several plays. A. A. Milne was well known as the author of "Winnie-the-Pooh", and the Christopher Robin verses, etc. E. C. Bentley was the inventor of the comic rhyming form known as the "Clerihew" – Clerihew was his middle name – and was the author, among other works, of a once famous detective story, "Trent's Last Case". Storm Jameson, Gilbert Frankau, Ethel Mannin, Dorothy Sayers, creator of the Lord Peter Wimsey detective novels, and Sax Rohmer, creator of Dr. Fu Manchu, were all popular novelists at the time. Monckton Hoffe was a successful dramatist, and Sean O'Casey a famous one, an Irishman with a reputation, then, of being fiercely anti-British though not of being pro-German. W. Townend is the same person who was at school with Wodehouse, and whose correspondence with him over 35 years is collected in "Performing Flea".

The first group of letters is from the Daily Telegraph. In order to convey the full and varied flavour of contemporary reaction to Wodehouse's release and broadcasts, at least as far as correspondents to the Daily Telegraph and The Times were concerned, all the letters published by them at the time are republished here:

"Sir – The news that P. G. Wodehouse had been released from his concentration camp delighted his friends; the news that he had settled down comfortably at the Adlon made them anxious; the news that he was to give weekly broadcasts (but not about politics, because he had "never taken any interest in politics") left them in no doubt as to what had happened to him. He had 'escaped' again.

"I remember that he told me once he wished he had a son; and he added characteristically (and quite sincerely): 'But he would have to be born at the age of 15, when he was just getting into his House eleven.' You see the advantage of that. Bringing up a son throws a considerable responsibility on a man; but by the time the boy is 15 one has shifted the responsibility on to the housemaster, without forfeiting any reflected glory that may be about.

"This, I felt, had always been Wodehouse's attitude to life. He has encouraged in himself a natural lack of interest in 'politics' – 'politics' being all the things which the grown-ups talk about at dinner when one is hiding under the table. Things, for instance, like the last war, which found and kept him in America; and post-war taxes, which chased him backwards and forwards across the Atlantic until he finally found sanctuary in France.

"An ill-chosen sanctuary it must have seemed last June, when politics came surging across the Somme.

"Irresponsibility in what the papers call 'a licensed humorist' can be carried too far; naîveté can be carried too far. Wodehouse has been given a good deal of licence in the past, but I fancy that now his licence will be withdrawn.

"Before this happens I beg him to surrender it of his own free will; to realise that though a genius may grant himself an enviable position about the battle where civic and social responsibilities are concerned, there are times when every man has to come down into the arena, pledge himself to the cause in which he believes, and suffer for it.

Yours &c., A. A. Milne."

"Sir – There is clearly only one opinion about Mr P. G. Wodehouse's bargain with the German Government; but those who feel most keenly on the subject, I should imagine, are the learned body responsible for conferring upon him the Oxford Doctorate of Letters in 1939.

15

"Oxford in recent years has been suffering from an attack of what may be called the 'Why-Shouldn't-I's'; and the most distressing symptom of it was the bestowal of one of the highest literary distinctions in the world upon one who has never written a serious line.

"Amends can be made, however. Those who awarded the honour can take the earliest opportunity of removing it. That action would have a certain effectiveness, not only as a mark of disapproval but as a sign of repentance; and most of my fellow-graduates, I believe, would heartily welcome it on both grounds.

Yours. &c., E. C. Bentley."

"Sir – The innumerable friends and admirers of P. G. Wodehouse must have rejoiced to hear that he has been released from long confinement in a Silesian internment camp and is now enjoying a modicum of personal liberty in Berlin. Wodehouse is nearly 60, and the strain of imprisonment has borne heavily upon him.

"We are less happy, however, at the news that he is to give a weekly broadcast from Berlin to America. To put it frankly, we are horrified.

"No broadcast from Berlin by a world-famous Englishman, however 'neutral' in tone, can serve as anything but an advertisement for Hitler; as a testimonial to Nazi toleration; as a shining instance of Nazi consideration and humanity towards prisoners of war – an ingenious dose, in other words, of soothing syrup for America, designed to divert American thoughts from the horrors which are being perpetrated in German prison camps today upon thousands of persons less happily situated than Mr. Wodehouse.

"There is no doubt that Wodehouse was deliberately released for this purpose. It was a brilliant idea, and unfortunately my old friend seems to have fallen for it. I have no hesitation in saying that he has not the slightest realisation of what he is doing. He is an easy-going and kindly man, cut off from public opinion here and with no one to advise him; and he probably agreed to broadcast because he saw no harm in the idea, and because, after long captivity, he is thus enabled to resume relations with his friends of the English-speaking world.

"But one thing is plain. No word of his can help our cause, and hardly any word can fail to help the enemy. The broadcasts must stop, for the sake of our country and for the sake of Wodehouse himself; for if he goes on he will lose every friend he has, and their name is legion.

"I therefore suggest that immediate steps should be taken through some friendly neutral authority in Berlin to drop a hint to our much-beloved but misguided 'Plum' to 'lay off'.

Your obedient servant, Ian Hay."

"Sir – I reckon myself to have been one of Mr. P. G. Wodehouse's earliest and most constant readers, but my devotion is certainly not proof against his Berlin performances.

"Almost the worst feature of the sorry business is the fact that he obviously has no idea that by giving his broadcasts he is committing moral and social suicide. Yet I believe it is true to say that if those Berlin broadcasts go on he will find himself, after the war, with scarcely a friend or reader left.

"Throughout life he has taken the easy and comfortable way. The beginning of the last war found him in America. He remained there, and amassed a comfortable fortune, while his friends fought. He was equally easy-going in his money affairs, for he came into the public eye later when the United States authorities demanded £50,000 of unpaid income tax from him.

"There were other tales. Indeed, one could hardly pass an hour in the company of those who saw Wodehouse often without being told of some new vagary. Because of their affection for him his friends condoned faults which they did not pretend to approve.

"But in allowing irresponsibility to carry him to the enemy's microphone he has at last gone too far. Who will be found to condone this crowning folly?

Yours &c., W. A. Darlington.

"Sir – Germany holds prisoner some 40,000 British soldiers and an English novelist. To the soldiers their country has given almost nothing but love and gratitude. To the novelist she has given almost everything. Yet he alone was willing to go to the microphone and let down the cause for which the 40,000 fought and suffered.

"Mr. P. G. Wodehouse, given his freedom and the right to stay at the Adlon Hotel, has told the world, in effect, that it does not matter who wins the war. Every time he feels 'any kind of belligerent feeling' creeping over him he meets 'a decent sort of chap' on the other side,

17

and realises that having a table and a typewriter (and presumably being able to stay at the Adlon and with friends in the country) are what matters.

"If he had spent the war in London or Bristol or Portsmouth, and helped to pull dead grandmothers and mutilated children from beneath wreckage, he might feel different. He might even have lost his typewriter and the table.

"Feeling as he does, one can only hope that in future he avoids a country that means so little to him and goes on playing Jeeves to Germans.

Yours truly, George Williams"

"Sir – So many letters in your much-read paper reveal pained surprise at P. G. Wodehouse's action. Why? Surely the mentality revealed in his books, amusing enough, I grant, would have led anyone to expect exactly what he has done.

Yours faithfully, L. B. Wilson."

"Sir – Today it would ill become anyone of Irish name to reproach even the feeblest of Britons with pusillanimity; but, as an English man of letters, senior by date of birth, and still more of publication, to all but a very few still on the active list of writers, I may beg leave to say that I consider Mr. Darlington's letter on the subject of a certain humorist's newest humour wholly and irreproachably to the point. It seems to me, on the evidence adduced, a most just indictment.

"As regards Oxford, I am old fashioned enough to take at their nominal value the words Honoris causa, if I sometimes wonder how some happy fellows, as the Prime Minister might say, 'owe so much to so little'.

"As regards Berlin – a graver matter – I can imagine that if Mr. Rudyard Kipling were with us still, he might write a fresh version of 'The Man Who Was' – which would indeed be quite another story.

Your obedient servant, Conal O'Riordan."

"Sir – It is amusing to read the various wails about the villainy of Wodehouse. The harm done to England's cause and to England's dignity is not the poor man's babble in Berlin, but the acceptance of him by a childish part of the people and the academic government of

18

Oxford, dead from the chin up, as a person of any importance what-soever in English humorous literature, or any literature at all. It is an ironic twist of retribution on those who banished Joyce and ho-noured Wodehouse.

"If England has any dignity left in the way of literature, she will forget for ever the pitiful antics of English Literature's performing flea. If Berlin thinks the poor fish great, so much the better for us.

Yours &c., Sean O'Casey."

"Sir – Pick up any book by Wodehouse and you find it peopled by men and women who have never worked and are moneyed and bored – the breeding ground for Fascism. For the embryo of the Fascist mentality was revealed in his whole set of characters, who were essentially undemocratic, unprogressive and reactionary.

"P. G. Wodehouse basked in the sun of his popularity and was lulled by the hum of the Drones Club whilst the armies of Europe massed. States were torn, and peoples crushed and oppressed. In his negligence lay his downfall; for every writer, every poet, and every artist who does not actively enlist his talents in this most vital revol-utionary struggle is against us – as much against us as if he were employed by Goebbels himself.

Yours sincerely, Colin Vincent."

"Sir – I loved Jeeves and Psmith, and cannot bear to associate their creator with the war-time Adlon. But facts must be faced. So it is 'Good-bye, Jeeves'.

Yours &c., H. S. S. Clarke."

"Sir – The Nazi expedient to use the propaganda value of a virtual appeal to the English-speaking public on both sides of the Atlantic by such a popular writer as Mr. P. G. Wodehouse is understand-able; but for that individual to allow his influence to be used in this way is despicable.

"The effect of popularity is often like that of an insidious poison if it is not kept under firm control; and one cannot help seeing in this a parallel case to that of Col. Lindbergh, which has done so much harm to the world democratic cause.

Yours faithfully, Charles Cunradi."

"Sir – Mr. W. A. Darlington's reference to a claim for £50,000 made by the United States Revenue upon P. G. Wodehouse is calculated to mislead. His view of the Berlin broadcasts one readily if sadly endorses; but I would like to point out that a similar claim (in my own case for a less staggering sum) was made upon all English novelists and playrights, or all of those with whom I am acquainted, who derived any considerable revenue from the U.S.A.

"These claims were based upon some obscure paragraph in the statute book hitherto overlooked even by the lawyers. Nevertheless assessment was made retrospective. Rafael Sabatini heroically took the matter to court and fought a losing action which dragged on for more than a year.

"In fairness to a man whose good name is at stake on other counts, I think the implication that Wodehouse's misfortune was due to conscious tax-dodging should be disclaimed.

Very faithfully yours, Sax Rohmer."

"Sir – It is to be noted that the popular national pastime of mud-slinging has promptly emerged from Mr. P. G. Wodehouse's indiscretion. One of your correspondents refers bitterly to the high honour that was conferred by Oxford University upon a mere humorist, and feels sure that his fellow-graduates would heartily welcome its rescinding, if only on that account alone.

"Another correspondent draws attention to the horrid fact that this creature once owed the United States a large sum of money – a rather unhappy allusion, one might suggest. Other dark deeds are merely hinted at in a vague but sinister manner. Walk up, ladies and gentlemen!

"There's someone in the stocks; let's fling a brick at him!

Yours faithfully, Monckton Hoffe."

"Sir – The discussion about Wodehouse is becoming sillier. The facts are that a wealthy and popular English novelist was caught by the Germans in France, found his imprisonment unendurable – it may have been painful as well as uncomfortable, but we don't know – and is now in the best hotel in Berlin. (One of your correspondents says that he is in the stocks. Obviously he does not know anything about the Adlon Hotel.)

"From here he is led or goes willingly to the microphone to tell the Americans what good fellows the Nazis are if you get on the right side of them or take the best view of them. It is a disgusting exhibition, and will remain just that, whatever the explanation, and whether or not we ought to be pitying Mr. Wodehouse for the sufferings which led him to prefer the Adlon.

"Judgment must be passed on the deed. We have as much right and duty to judge it as to judge the deeds of a Quisling. We need not judge the man. Leave that to the Spirit of the Pities, or the Spirits Sinister and Ironic.

"The suggestion that Oxford ought to withdraw the degree it conferred on him is tactless. It was, I think, Caligula who made his horse a Senator. Probably the horse was charming and probably the other Senators preferred not to notice him. Why not allow a foolish and frivolous gesture to be forgotten?

Yours, &c., Storm Jameson."

"Sir – Are Plum Wodehouse's self-righteous colleagues of the pen so sure that they themselves might not have yielded to a similar temptation? The Hun has means of persuasion which are not known to the willow-wielding gentlemen of Oxford and Cambridge.

"One asks oneself how much of this heresy-hunt is due to jealousy of Plum's capacity for money-making: and whether it will eventually include our more astute litterati who removed themselves, their tables and their typewriters to the other side of the Atlantic.

"A poor blood sport at best!

Yours &c., Gilbert Frankau."

"Sir – As a very old friend and admirer of P. G. Wodehouse – known to his intimates as 'Plummy' – I entirely agree with Ian Hay when he says that 'P. G.' has not the slightest realisation of what he is doing.

"He is a man that mundane matters seem not to affect. He always appears vague in conversation and seems to be thinking of something else. I consider that Ian Hay's suggestion is an excellent one – that steps should be taken through some friendly neutral authority in Berlin to explain to him the enormity of what he is doing.

"If I know 'Plummy', he will assuredly awake and realise the criminal folly of his action and, as Ian Hay puts it, 'lay off'.

Yours faithfully, (Lord) Newborough."

"Sir – Since some fellow-authors have seen fit to censure P. G. Wodehouse in a 'We-wouldn't-do-that-sort-of-thing' manner, may I suggest that judgment be withheld, since we are none of us in a position to know the facts?

"It is always difficult to gauge another person's motives; how can any of us say with certainty what we would do in given circumstances? None of the people so busily censuring Mr. Wodehouse has had his experiences. I was always under the impression that part of the Christian ethic was 'Judge not that ye be not judged'.

"A great spate of censure was released on the head of King Leopold after the capitulation of Belgium. Now a whitewashing campaign is afoot, for judgment, it seems, was too hastily passed. The case of Mr. Wodehouse is hardly a national affair (if I may say so), and it might well be that he is being misjudged. Must we pass judgment in any case? And is the matter all that important in a world war?

Yours faithfully, Ethel Mannin."

"Sir – Some of your distinguished correspondents writing about Mr. Wodehouse's lapse become astonishingly pompous. Mr. A. A. Milne suggests that Wodehouse has always been an irresponsible 'escapist', while Mr. E. C. Bentley is upset that an Oxford D.Litt. should ever have been given to a man 'who has never written a serious line'.

"But both seem to expect from Mr. Wodehouse, after his – in their view – consistent record of irresponsible buffoonery, an entirely adamantine and stoical behaviour after a dose of German imprisonment. On their estimate of his character it seems a lot to ask.

"As for the charge that these broadcasts harm our cause in the United States, we may wonder whether the Americans will be greatly moved by Wodehousian 'goofiness' from Berlin when they have been left cold by the arguments of their own one-time idol, Col. Lindbergh, who has also accepted Nazi hospitality. By keeping all our anger for the Nazis we shall show a better sense of humour than by addressing to our own weaker brethren moral lectures which they will not be allowed to read.

Yours &c., Walter James."

"Sir – In the discussion about P. G. Wodehouse's unhappy broadcasts, there is one point of which we ought, I think, to remind ourselves. At the time of the Battle of France, when he fell into enemy hands, English people had scarcely begun to realise the military and political importance of the German propaganda weapon. Since then we have learned much. We know something of why and how France fell; we have seen disintegration at work in the Balkans; we have watched the slow recovery of American opinion from the influence of the Nazi hypnotic.

"But how much of all this can possibly be known or appreciated from inside a German concentration camp – or even from the Adlon Hotel? Theoretically, no doubt, every patriotic person should be prepared to resist enemy pressure to the point of martyrdom; but it must be far more difficult to bear such heroic witness when its urgent necessity is not, and cannot be, understood.

Yours faithfully, Dorothy L. Sayers."

"Sir – No writer has ever sought publicity less than P. G. Wodehouse. As his oldest friend, I can testify that to no writer has publicity ever done more harm.

"When the last war broke out he had settled in New York. In April 1917, when the United States entered the war, a recruiting office was set up for Britons resident in that country. Wodehouse offered himself for enlistment and was medically rejected as quite unfit for military service.

"That he had trouble over his income-tax has often been brought up against him. As Mr. W. A. Darlington says, the U.S. Government demanded £50,000 of unpaid income-tax from him. What Mr. Darlington omits to say is that the U.S. Government after prolonged negotiation accepted one-seventh the sum originally asked for. Had the larger amount been proven legally theirs, they would not have accepted the smaller.

"A comparison of any picture taken of Plum Wodehouse before the war and one taken in Silesia will show what long months of confinement on prison fare have done for him. Let us, before we cast stones, seek to understand his predicament and help him in turn to understand that for his own sake, his family's sake, and his country's sake his broadcasts must stop. But how is that vital message to reach him?

Your obedient servant, W. Townend."

"Sir – Mr. Sean O'Casey mentions 'those who banished Joyce and honoured Wodehouse'. May we take it he means James Joyce not William?

Yours &c., Jack Point."

"Sir – In view of the letters you have received about Mr. P. G. Wodehouse, it may be of interest to know the facts surrounding his release from prison camp which have just come into my possession.

"Mr. Wodehouse was captured last year because he refused to believe that the Germans were approaching his residence where he was working on a book. He wished to finish the last four chapters before leaving France. At that time he was over 58. The Germans are not interning enemy aliens over 60, and Mr. Wodehouse will be 60 within a few months.

"The camp in which he was imprisoned is one of the best in Germany. A former asylum for the insane, its accommodation is comfortable, and its commanding officer, a British prisoner during the last war, moderate and lenient. Although he was offered a room to himself, Mr. Wodehouse refused to accept preferential treatment, and shared a room with 60 others. He was, however, given space in which to write. This was a large room in which a tap-dancer, a saxophonist and a pianist were also 'working'.

"The Columbia Broadcasting Co. and several other American agencies had been in touch with Mr. Wodehouse for some time with a view to securing his stories. His broadcasts for Columbia were arranged before he left the prison camp, and set for whatever time he might be released in the normal course of events. This came within a short time of his 60th birthday.

"Released prisoners are free to live where they choose within central districts. Mr. Wodehouse's considerable royalties from his books published in Germany undoubtedly decided him to select the greater comfort of the Adlon in preference to more modest accommodation elsewhere in the centre of Berlin.

"I have no right or desire to comment or pass judgment on Mr. Wodehouse's action, but I would add the remarks made by some who knew him in Berlin. They agree with Mr. A. A. Milne that he is politically naïve, and with Miss Dorothy Sayers that he is unconscious of the propaganda value to the Germans of his action. It sprang, they say, from his desire to keep his name before his American reading public. But they do add, most emphatically, that he did not buy his release from prison camp by agreeing to broadcast. Anxiety for his wife, whom he had left near Lille, may have led him to press for release several weeks before it would normally have been granted him.

"The fact that his 'money sense' may, and apparently does, exceed his patriotic sense can scarcely place him in a favourable light; but the position is perhaps altered slightly by the circumstances surrounding his release.

Yours faithfully, Disinterested."

The letters in The Times, which appeared between 18th and 23rd July 1941, were concerned less with Wodehouse's broadcasts themselves than with the response by "Cassandra" on the B.B.C. However, they also contain a letter from Duff Cooper taking responsibility for that broadcast, and one by "Cassandra" himself. The whole correspondence reads as follows:

"Sir – I feel certain that I shall not be the first, but I should like to the among those who will most surely voice their protest against any repetition of such an example of appallingly bad taste as that exhibited by the B.B.C. after the nine o'clock news last evening in allowing the 'indictment' of P. G. Wodehouse given by a male-voiced Cassandra who, I understood from the announcement, has some connexion with the Daily Mirror.

"The recent behaviour of P. G. Wodehouse is, of course, indefensible, but surely the best way to treat such unfortunate incidents has already been demonstrated when the case in question was raised in the House a few days ago. A straightforward and concise explanation and, if thought fit, a suitable denunciation would have been sufficient to clear the matter before a public which may have gathered the wrong impression from scanty reports and rumours; the whole affair could then most happily be forgotten. There is no argument in support of nearly ten minutes of irrelevant sneering pseudo-dramatically delivered. Even to those who have never appreciated Wodehouse's humour, it was merely embarrassing.

Yours &c., Ronald F. Barraud."

"The following are extracts from a large number of letters which have reached The Times on the subject of a recent B.B.C. Postscript:

"I hope that some more powerful voice than mine will be raised to protest against the malicious piece of vulgarity presented to us by the B.B.C. Strange as it may appear to the Picture Press, I believe that the majority of decent people are interested in the writings and not in the private lives of prominent living writers, and that they are not in danger of thinking either too much or too little of them whatever the honour done them by public academic bodies. Not the least distressing features of the broadcast were the vindictive accents of the speaker and his rather cheap attempt to copy the methods of Mr. Quentin Reynolds. – Mr. C. A. Whitton."

"I feel I am expressing the opinion of many people in protesting against the postscript on P. G. Wodehouse given after the nine o'clock news by Cassandra. Personal abuse like this, whatever the merits of the case, serves to lower the standard of B.B.C. broadcasts – usually so high. Surely we do not need to imitate the style of the Nazis. – Mrs. Denys Danby."

"Will you allow me space to protest against the broadcasting by the B.B.C. after the nine o'clock news of the recording by Cassandra? I think I have never heard a meaner piece of invective given such publicity before all the facts and circumstances are known on which a fair judgment might be formed. – Mr. A. Guy Moore."

"I trust that the broadcast made last night by Cassandra will not be taken as creating a precedent. I am sure that many people were amazed that the B.B.C. should have allowed itself to be made the medium for the dissemination of such an item. – Mr. S. E. Gillett."

"The B.B.C. maintains a very high level of Postscripts. Who was responsible for Cassandra's amazing broadcast about P. G. Wodehouse? Anyone who thinks Wodehouse's political opinions are important to the world can be only a little more simple than Mr. Wodehouse himself. Cassandra, copying Mr. Quentin Reynolds in manner but in nothing else, delivered himself of a petty, degrading, and ill-proportioned sneer. Beginning with a sneer at Wodehouse for gambling, he ended with a sneer at his quite unexceptionable Christian names. Was this performance sponsored by the Foreign Office or the Ministry of Information?–　　　　　A Serving Officer."

"Sir – In justice to the Governors of the B.B.C. I must make it plain that mine was the sole responsibility for the broadcast which last week distressed so many of your readers. The Governors indeed shared unanimously the view expressed in your columns that the broadcast in question was in execrable taste. *De gustibus non est disputandum.* Occasions, however, may arise in time of war when plain speaking is more desirable than good taste.

　　　　　I am, Sir, your obedient servant, Duff Cooper."

"Sir – I had not intended to intervene in the controversy about my recent broadcast on the subject of P. G. Wodehouse, but the relish and the perseverance with which you seek to discredit me necessitates an answer. I have been condemned on the grounds of bad taste. Since when has it been bad taste to name and nail a traitor to England? The letters which you have published have only served as a sad demonstration that there is still in this country a section of the community eager and willing to defend its own quislings.

"You claim that there has been a 'storm of protest' against this talk. I wonder. Of the letters received by the Daily Mirror over 90 per cent have completely approved of what I said. The remainder expressed the point of view to which you have given so much publicity. The correspondents of the Daily Mirror are not yours, but as a sample of general public opinion they are far more reliable than any mass readership index to which The Times may lay claim. By pure reasons of circulation they come from a representative slice of the community which outnumbers your readership by 10 to 1. The people who approved of what I said about P. G. Wodehouse are pre-eminently among the vast masses of fighting men, factory workers, miners, and the ordinary common people who are carrying the burden of this war. However, I do not begrudge you the 'storm of protest' which you have so diligently fanned, for it compares favourably with the flat calm of acquiescence which was such a prominent feature of your correspondence before and up to the year of Munich.

"I learn with interest that the Governors of the B.B.C. share your views of what you describe as a 'notorious' broadcast. However, I accurately anticipated their reaction and it is to the credit of Mr. Duff Cooper that he insisted beforehand that the B.B.C. should have no say whatsoever in the script of this talk. It would certainly not have been possible for him to have adopted this point of view, had it not been that their lamentable Governorship had rendered matters of propaganda demonstrably outside their scope.

"To the accusation that this broadcast was vulgar, I would remind you that this is a vulgar war, in which our countrymen are being killed by the enemy without regard to good form or bad taste. When Dr. Goebbels announces an apparently new and willing propaganda-recruit to further this slaughter I still retain the right to denounce this treachery in terms compatible with my own conscience – and nothing else.

Yours faithfully, William N. Connor ('Cassandra')."

Feeling against Wodehouse certainly ran high in many quarters. For example, Southport Public Library removed 90 Wodehouse books from their shelves and destroyed them. Other public libraries refused to buy any more Wodehouse books. The B.B.C. banned all his works. However, it is worth noting that, in spite of all this, no less than 450,00 copies of Wodehouse's books were sold in the United Kingdom between 1941 and the end of the war.

After Cassandra's broadcast, almost all British national newspapers took it as accepted fact that Wodehouse was indeed a collaborator at best; at worst, a traitor. In the British press from June 1941 onwards, Wodehouse was commonly referred to as "a Nazi stooge" or "a Goebbels stooge". He was the "man who let down his country", who "agreed to thank the Nazis (for his release) by broadcasting", who "had cracked his worst joke", whose "behaviour is indefensible". To the Sunday Express, on 27th July 1941, he was simply "a fool or a louse". The Empire News added to the charges of collaboration with the Nazis that of "sneering at the French and the Belgians" in his Berlin broadcasts. A columnist in the Daily Express wrote about Wodehouse's life in Germany after his release from Tost: "Life in hell is good to live, I guess, if you are Mr. Lucifer's personal guest." On 1st December 1944, the News Chronicle printed a report of an alleged incident when two British officers were drinking in a Paris café, when they were approached by an elderly man, who entered into conversation with them. After some minutes, the elderly man asked: "What do they think of Wodehouse in England?" To this, one of the officers replied: "In England his name stinks." Whereupon the elderly man went pale, and immediately left. The two officers then realised they had been speaking to Wodehouse himself.

Furthermore, the most fantastic stories were fabricated and widely believed. For example, it was printed as unqualified fact that he received pocket-money from the Germans and was given special exchange rates by them. On 20th November 1944 the newspaper, Reynolds News, printed a story which it had picked up from Paris Radio, under the headline "Wodehouse Insulted Britons", which read: "Broadcasts made by P. G. Wodehouse, the novelist, over the German Radio, insulted both the French Resistance Movement and the British people, Paris Radio said last night.

"In one broadcast he said that he had discovered when 'detained' by the Germans that all the British rounded up by the Germans in France in 1940 were not 'real British, but either Russians, Poles or Jews'.

"French patriots fighting against Petain and the Nazis he described as 'Paris apaches and pimps'."

In the case of at least the first part of this absurdly false story it is possible, and instructive, to trace it to its harmless origins. These origins were not, as Paris Radio and Reynolds News claimed, one of Wodehouse's broadcasts, but an article he wrote while in internment – part, as he wrote, of "my efforts, during the first few weeks of transplantation from home, to preserve a stiff upper lip" – an article which was published in the Saturday Evening Post and reprinted in part in the United Kingdom in the Daily Mail of 17th July 1941:

"Since 21st July 1940, I have been a guest of the German Government at a series of their justly popular internment camps (remind me to tell you sometime of a week I spent in Loos Prison. Oh, Baby!), and at this moment the whole world, you might say, is seeking an answer to the question: What is going to be the effect on Wodehouse of this spell in the cooler? Have we got to go back to the same old codger we've seen tottering around these last 60 years or so, or will there emerge something new and unforeseen . . .

"We will begin by dividing Wodehouse into sections, as I am convinced the crews of the German bombers were saying to themselves when they dropped their bombs that morning last May in the vicinity of my villa at Le Touquet.

"There is (1) Wodehouse, the man; (2) Wodehouse, the Englishman; (3) Wodehouse, the idol of society . . ."

Wodehouse first deals with the changes in "Wodehouse, the man", touching on the advantages and disadvantages of beards, and then turns to "Wodehouse, the Englishman": "Here the change in me will be spiritual rather than physical, and it will be a very great change. In the days before the war I had always been modestly proud of being an Englishman, but now that I have been for some months resident in this bin or repository for Englishmen I am not so sure.

"The fact is, if you throw a dragnet over France, Poland, Norway, Belgium and Holland, scooping in everything with a British identity card, you would get an odd catch. Here an Englishman may be anything from a Borneo head-hunter to the son of a Bulgarian of Indo-Chinese parentage.

"I am pretty sure several of us are baboons, and it is here I feel the line should be drawn. If an internee has a tail he should be given his freedom."

Such was the innocent origin of the vicious falsehood promoted by Paris Radio and Reynolds News.

In the United States, also, the allegations of contemptible behaviour by Wodehouse were believed and promulgated. The American newspaper, P.M., on 2nd July 1941, in an article that appeared under the headline "Wodehouse Plays Jeeves to Nazis," wrote: "He seems a complete egotist. He seems to figure that these broadcasts are a small price for winning the limited freedom of war-time Berlin in place of an internment camp.

"But, come to think of it, he probably would be shocked if you accused him of betraying his country. He'd probably answer, 'Well now, that's a bit rough. I was only trying to be amusing.' " A typical story in the New York Times, on 16th September 1942, described Wodehouse as having been taken prisoner by the Germans, and having afterwards "accepted German hospitality on a luxurious scale". On 20th June 1943, the same newspaper wrote that Wodehouse had been "installed at the Adlon Hotel in Berlin at the expense of the German Government". And again on 21st August 1944, going even further down the road of false rumour, the New York

Times described Wodehouse as having "broadcast from Berlin advocating a separate peace".

It must be emphasised that, of course, not everyone accepted that Wodehouse was guilty of the charges of collaboration and cowardice. There were certainly letters, as quoted above, to the British press deploring the vilification of Wodehouse, pointing out, in the traditional spirit of British justice, that he was being condemned without having a chance to defend himself. The Thurrock local council, in Essex, voted positively against banning Wodehouse's books from their public library. But such public attitudes were in the minority. To the public at large, Wodehouse became, beyond doubt, a collaborator or traitor.

And although, after the war was over, time blunted the edge of public anger, in the eyes of many he remained a traitor. In 1954, one American book reviewer wrote " . . . his (Wodehouse's) Nazi captors persuaded him to broadcast from his Upper Silesia prison, an appeal to his British countrymen to surrender to the Madman of Berchtesgaden." Again, one senior British statesman said to me as late as 1980, "Oh yes, I know all about the Wodehouse case. The man was an out-and-out traitor. He was anti-Churchill. He broadcast propaganda for the Nazis."

*   *   *

Apart from patriotic disgust at what Wodehouse was alleged to have done, there was a further reason behind the attacks on Wodehouse in certain sections of the British war-time media, and this was an ideological one. Those in Britain who were disgusted at what they believed to be Wodehouse's behaviour, were not, of course, confined to any one political party. For example, the Minister of Information, Duff Cooper, was a Conservative M.P. of a traditionalist kind, whereas the journalist William Connor was a robust supporter of the Labour Party. None the less, among various left-wing political groups and individuals, there was a sustained attempt, from the time of Wodehouse's Berlin broadcasts onwards, to portray Wodehouse's alleged action not merely as the aberration of a contemptible individual, but as being somehow typical of his "class". The fact – as it was taken by such left-wing groups and individuals – of Wodehouse's treachery was tied to the fact that Wodehouse himself was rich – ignoring the fact that he had worked hard for every penny – and that he wrote frequently about the British aristocracy. Cassandra in his broadcast of 15th July 1941, parts of which have already been quoted, emphasised the fact that Wodehouse was "rich", that he was a "playboy" and a "gambler", and that his two Christian names were the aristocratic-sounding ones, "Pelham Grenville".

George Orwell, a Socialist, even if a somewhat maverick one, first pointed out in 1945, in his essay "In Defence of P. G. Wodehouse", that Wodehouse, being rich, and associated in the public mind with the idle, aristocratic characters he frequently wrote about, "made an ideal whipping boy" for the Left.

Evelyn Waugh – who, unlike Orwell, was a romantic Conservative – in his broadcast about Wodehouse on the B.B.C. of 15th July 1961, called in evidence the correspondent in the Daily Telegraph, Colin Vincent, whose letter has already been quoted in this book, as being one man, typical of many on the Left who "led the hunt beyond the author to these (Wodehouse's) characters, whom he (Vincent) described as 'moneyed and bored – the breeding ground of Fascism . . . The embryo of the Fascist mentality' he said 'was revealed in his (Wodehouse's) whole set of characters'. The conception of Mr. Mulliner and Lord Emsworth as potential Eichmanns would be too grotesque to deserve mention were it not a symptom of that diseased period. In England, as in other countries during the last war, there were men and women who sought to direct the struggle for national survival into proletarian revolution . . ."

A clear example of what Orwell and Waugh meant by the attempt of the Left in war-time Britain to link the concept of treachery with the so-called "ruling classes", appeared in the British Communist newspaper, the Daily Worker, on 24th November 1944: "P. G. Wodehouse, it seems, got on a lot better with the Germans than with the French. This despicable Englishman, who was described by Mr. Eden as having 'lent his services to the German propaganda machine,' is under investigation by the French police.

"The friends of Wodehouse in this country – the wealthy can always find supporters in the Press – have raised vociferous voices in his defence.

"Poor harmless, little chap, he really did not know what he was doing. He is amiable and boneheaded, says the Daily Mail.

"We do not dispute that Wodehouse is as petty and contemptible as the ruling-class characters portrayed in his best-sellers. But since when has amiability and boneheadedness been an excuse for serving Goebbels?

"The sloppy Wodehouse broadcasts from Berlin were deliberately selected by the subtle German propagandists. Better a famous British author expressing doubts about the victory of his own country than a second Haw-Haw churning out fantastic lies.

"Wodehouse represents the rottenness that infected a section of Britain in the years preceding the war. His day is over."

＊　　＊　　＊

The role of the B.B.C. in the Wodehouse affair is worth examining in some detail. Because the broadcast by Cassandra went out on the B.B.C. Home Service on 15th July 1941, immediately after the nine o'clock news, what was said about Wodehouse was invested with all the attributes of reliability which normally attached to the B.B.C. itself. Wodehouse was widely believed to be a traitor because he had been called a traitor on the B.B.C. But in fact, the B.B.C. had not been responsible for Cassandra's broadcast. What had happened was this: the B.B.C. was required, under war-time regulations, to make time available to the Ministry of Information for Government propaganda. The ten minutes occupied by the Cassandra broadcast on 15th July was such a time. Thus the standards of the broadcast were not those of the B.B.C., but of Government propaganda as written and spoken by a brilliantly sulphurous journalist. The Governors of the B.B.C., as a body, officially told Duff Cooper, as Minister of Information, that the proposed Cassandra broadcast would be unwise, as they, the B.B.C., had monitored the first two Wodehouse broadcasts – the others were not broadcast until after 15th July – and that they were innocuous from the point of view of politics or propaganda. It was certainly clear to the Governors of the B.B.C., even at that early stage, that Wodehouse was no "Lord Haw-Haw". In his broadcast of 15th July 1961 on the B.B.C. to celebrate Wodehouse's 80th birthday, already mentioned, Evelyn Waugh said of this aspect of the affair: "Let it be said that no one connected with the B.B.C. had any responsibility for this utterance (the Cassandra broadcast). It was concocted over the luncheon table by the Minister of Information (Duff Cooper) and the journalist (William Connor). All the Governors formally protested against it; one of them, I believe, who was a friend of the Prime Minister of the time (Winston Churchill) went to him personally to ask him to over-ride his Minister's judgment. They were rebuffed, and the incident provides a glaring example of the danger of allowing politicians to control public communication . . ."

But although the B.B.C. can fairly claim innocence at this stage, it could not do so later. On 22nd December 1943 it was announced by the B.B.C. that because of Wodehouse's broadcasts from Berlin, his work, as noted earlier, was to be banned on the B.B.C. – the ban extending even to songs with his lyrics. In a letter to Townend in 1950, Wodehouse refers to this ban: "By the way, I have just heard from Watt (his London agent) that the B.B.C. want to do my 'Damsel in Distress' on their Light Programme. Always up to now they have told him that nothing by P. G. Wodehouse would even be considered. Well, what I'm driving at is that I had always said to myself: 'One of these days the B.B.C. will come asking for something of mine, and then won't I just draw myself up to my full height and write them a stinker saying that after what has occurred I am amazed – nay astounded – at their crust – etc. etc.' Of course what actually happened was that I wrote to Watt saying Okay, go ahead."

There is a passage, relevant to the question of what was the true attitude of the B.B.C. itself, in the diaries of Sir (then Mr.) Harold Nicolson. Nicolson was a Governor of the B.B.C. from 1941 to 1946 and a National Labour Member of Parliament throughout the Second World War. He was a junior Minister at the Ministry of Information from 1940 to 1941 and was in fact dismissed by Churchill only a week after the Cassandra broadcast, at the same time as Duff Cooper was also removed as Minister of Information. In his diary of 4th January 1944 Nicolson wrote: "I got a letter today from John Masefield, as President of the Incorporated Society of Authors, etc., asking me (as a Governor of the B.B.C.) why the B.B.C. have 'banned' Wodehouse. If anybody we do not want to employ is regarded as 'banned', then the B.B.C. will lose all freedom of selection.

Moreover, there is no doubt that Wodehouse allowed himself for a 'consideration' to be used for broadcasts which were in the interests of the enemy. As such he is a traitor and should not be used. I do not want to see Wodehouse shot on Tower Hill. But I resent the theory that 'poor P.G. is so innocent that he is not responsible'. A man who has shown such ingenuity and resource in evading British and American income tax cannot be classed as unpractical." (This passage was not included in the relevant volume of Nicolson's diaries published during Wodehouse's lifetime, but was included in the later, one-volume edition, which first appeared in 1980.)

At the time of the Adjournment Debate on Wodehouse in the House of Commons on 15th December 1944, Nicolson wrote in a letter to his son, Nigel, then serving in Italy with the Grenadier Guards: "The Attorney-General (Sir Donald Somervell) was much embarrassed by my intervention (in the debate). I admit that to accuse Wodehouse of High Treason is to employ a steam-hammer to crush a louse. I only intervened as I do not want people to imagine Wodehouse has been declared innocent."

On 22nd December 1944, in one of the weekly articles, entitled Marginal Comment, which Nicolson was writing for the Spectator magazine at the time, his comments on Wodehouse are somewhat milder: "I am assured, however, by those who know Mr. Wodehouse that he is a child in all such matters (i.e. politics and propaganda) and that his irresponsibility in mundane affairs has to be seen to be believed . . ." (Nicolson himself hardly knew Wodehouse and was not an admirer of his work, according to his son, Nigel.) Nicolson concludes that ". . . Reasonable people will conclude that they (the facts of the Berlin broadcasts as selected and set out in the Spectator article by Nicolson) are not, after all, so very bad; they will also agree that even under the most charitable interpretation they are not so very good. And the best thing is to do nothing."

It is interesting to note, further to the true attitude of the B.B.C. to Wodehouse, that in 1961, when the author Christopher Sykes, who was both a B.B.C. producer and a friend and biographer of Evelyn Waugh, was trying to persuade the B.B.C. to allow Waugh to broadcast about Wodehouse to celebrate his, Wodehouse's, 80th birthday, he, Sykes, found great difficulty in persuading them to do so. In his biography of Waugh, Sykes wrote: "I found that 'Cassandra's' propaganda had stuck. I found it was believed that Wodehouse *was* a traitor, and that it would be unworthy of the B.B.C. to pay honour to such a malefactor except in the most detached spirit of literary criticism. I found that presentation of the facts made little impression, and that Evelyn (Waugh's) proposal was interpreted as an attempt to make the B.B.C. offer an abject apology for having performed a necessary duty . . ."

As far as the actions of Duff Cooper (later Lord Norwich) and William Connor (later Sir William) were concerned, it must be said that both men, at the time, believed that what was broadcast on the programme of 15th July 1941 was strictly truthful, and that, in ensuring that it was broadcast, they were fulfilling an important patriotic duty.

Long after the war, Connor came to believe that Wodehouse was innocent and made a full and generous apology to him.

Duff Cooper, however, never apologised. In a letter to me of 18th March 1981, Duff Cooper's son, Lord Norwich, wrote: ". . . I scarcely ever remember my father talking about it (the Wodehouse affair). What I do know, however, is that his reasons for acting as he did were entirely prompted by the fact that Wodehouse's broadcasts were beamed at America; this was at a time when we were very anxious to stiffen up the Americans – isolationism, as you remember, was rife – and my father felt that it was dangerous for the Americans to be told by a famous and respected figure that he was living very comfortably in Germany, and that the Germans were very nice chaps who looked after him admirably.

"Whether or not he revised his opinion in later life I am unable to say; I have no reason to think he did. He was, however, always a great admirer of Wodehouse as a writer, and I also remember him saying on one occasion that, much as he objected to the broadcasts, he believed that Wodehouse had never written anything better."

*　　*　　*

In Malcolm Muggeridge's essay on the Wodehouse affair, published in the volume entitled "Tread Softly For You Tread on My Jokes", Muggeridge describes how he visited Duff Cooper in Paris in 1944, where Cooper was then British Ambassador. According to Muggeridge, Cooper said to him that Wodehouse "had always evaded reality and his responsibilities as a citizen". This charge of the evasion of responsiblities appears to refer to Cooper's belief, and to the belief of others already quoted, that Wodehouse had managed to evade fighting in the First World War, and that he owed the U.S. Inland Revenue Service substantial amounts of unpaid income tax, and had contrived to pay as little British tax as possible for many years.

Regarding the charge that Wodehouse did not fight in the First World War, it is indeed true. But the reasons why it is true, show no evasion of responsibility. In 1914, at the age of 32, Wodehouse tried to enlist in the Royal Navy. But he was rejected because of his poor eyesight. Wodehouse then tried again to enlist in New York, when a recruiting office for Britons abroad was opened there, in 1917. Again he was rejected and for the same reason.

As far as Duff Cooper's, and others' comments about "irresponsibility" over tax matters are concerned, the implications of these comments are, in one instance, somewhat unfair, and in another, wholly false. It was, in fact, Ethel Wodehouse who insisted on their travels to avoid, perfectly legally, paying more tax than was necessary to both British and American authorities. Ethel liked having plenty of money – not least to pay for her gambling. Nonetheless, Wodehouse must bear responsibility in that he acquiesced.

Regarding the charge, referred to implicitly by Duff Cooper and others, that he illegally evaded United States income tax – the U.S. authorities in 1934 were demanding some $50,000 from him – this charge was false. The facts were set out by Wodehouse's fellow author Sax Rohmer in the letter to the Daily Telegraph of July 1941, already quoted. In summary, Rohmer explained that it was not just Wodehouse who suddenly received massive demands from the U.S. Inland Revenue, for past taxes allegedly not paid: every single British novelist and playwright, who earned revenue in the United States, received a similar back-dated demand. In the end this particular tax demand was settled amicably, as Wodehouse's friend, Bill Townend, pointed out in his letter to the Daily Telegraph, with the U.S. authorities accepting only one-seventh of what they had originally demanded from Wodehouse. But in 1945 they suddenly claimed that Wodehouse had paid no U.S. taxes in 1923 and 1924. It was extremely difficult for Wodehouse, then in war-time Paris, to prove that he had duly paid his taxes some twenty years previously.

As he wrote to Bill Townend on 22nd May 1945: 'I have absolutely no means of proving that I did (pay my taxes), but I must have done. I was in America both years and left for England, and you can't get on a boat at New York unless you show that you have paid your income tax. I suppose that what will happen is that after I have spent thousands of dollars on lawyers' fees they will drop the thing. But it's an awful nuisance, and I wouldn't have thought that legally they were entitled to go back twenty-two years. But they just make up the rules as they go along. It reminds me of George Ade's story of the man who was in prison and a friend went to see him and asked what he had done. The man told him and the friend said, 'But they can't put you in prison for that', and the man said, 'I know they can't, but they have'." Eventually, after having impounded all Wodehouse's money in the United States, the U.S. Tax Court decided in 1947 that Wodehouse had indeed paid his due taxes. As Wodehouse wrote to Townend on 12th April 1947: " .. The net result of the various (Wodehouse tax) cases is they (U.S. tax authorities) will stick to about $20,000 and I shall get a refund of about $19,000, and the extraordinary thing is that instead of mourning over the lost $20,000, I am feeling frightfully rich, as if I had just been left $19,000 by an uncle in Australia. I find nowadays that any cash these Governments allow me to keep seems like money for jam."

*　　*　　*

The main charges against Wodehouse must now be examined in turn, in the light of the evidence collected by Cussen in 1944 and 1945, and in light of the evidence which has been uncovered since then.

The first charge was that Wodehouse made no attempt to escape from Le Touquet, where he was living in 1940, in the face of the advancing German army. This charge was false. In fact, the Wodehouses made two attempts to escape, having taken what seemed to them all reasonable steps in the circumstances to obtain official advice as to if, and when, to leave. What happened was as follows:

On Monday, 20th May 1940, the Wodehouses decided they would have to leave Le Touquet. The reason that they had not tried to escape earlier was because they had not believed it would be necessary: nearly everyone, military and civilian, badly misjudged the speed and success of the German advance. The Wodehouses were understandably reluctant to flee and abandon their house, leaving it and its contents unprotected if, in fact, the Germans were going to be halted, as they hoped and expected. The Wodehouses therefore refused to panic and made formal arrangements with the British Vice-Consul at Boulogne to let them know in good time if ever it should be necessary to leave Le Touquet.

Evidence to this effect came from the questioning by Cussen of an Austrian national, Freddie Kraus, arrested by the Allies in Paris in 1944, who had first met the Wodehouses in Paris in December 1943, and frequently thereafter. Kraus told Cussen: "... He (Wodehouse) and his wife had arranged with the English (sic) Consul in Le Touquet in May 1940 that the latter would let Wodehouse know in good time should the Germans advance further, in order that Wodehouse would be able to get away in good time to England. He was just listening to the B.B.C. news, stating that the Germans had been thrown back, when the first German soldiers appeared ... "

In fact there was no British Consul at Le Touquet. Jacqueline Grant (later Mrs Powell), daughter of Arthur Grant, the golf professional at Le Touquet in 1940, told me in 1981 that the Wodehouse's had indeed tried to make such arrangements with consular officials, as Kraus had said, but that the official was in fact the British Vice-Consul at Boulogne. Jacqueline Grant was secretary to Ethel Wodehouse in May 1940, and the Grant family were neighbours and good friends of the Wodehouses. Mrs. Ruth Grant, Jacqueine's mother, kept a diary, and also fuller written accounts, of events at the time: these confirm in detail Wodehouse's statement about how they tried to escape.

In the event, none of the British residents at Le Touquet, including the Wodehouses, received any advice about the true nature of the German advance from British consular officials. At the time, British residents were bitter about this lack of warning, but later they realised it was almost certainly due not to incompetence so much as to ignorance in official circles as to what exactly was happening.

In addition to this official contact with the British Vice-Consul at Boulogne, the Wodehouses could have expected to get any warning that might have been available from two other British sources, with whom they were on friendly terms: first, from the Commanding Officer of the British Military Hospital at Étaples; and second, from members of 85 Squadron of the Royal Air Force, which was then stationed in the area. In his evidence to Cussen, Wodehouse said: "We saw a great deal at this time of Squadron No. 85 of the R.A.F., members of which were a great deal round at our house, and we would also go to dinner parties with them." Jacqueline Grant confirmed to me that Ethel Wodehouse was extremely generous with her hospitality to British military personnel in the area, seeing such hospitality by her as a contribution to the morale of the armed services. None of the advice which the Wodehouses received, as Jacqueline Grant confirmed to me, either from the Vice-Consul or from their friends in the British armed forces, was to the effect that they should leave Le Touquet earlier than they attempted.

Some British residents in Le Touquet did indeed flee long before 20th May, but the Wodehouses, like the Grants, regarded this as an unjustified and unworthy panic. They believed that the British and French forces would halt the German advance long before Le Touquet was threatened. It is an irony that their behaviour in staying put, which was rightly regarded at the time as showing considerable courage, and faith in the British ability to contain the Germans, should later have been misinterpreted as being evidence of welcoming the German military successes.

In addition to any advice the Wodehouses had from British sources, they also had two French military doctors billeted with them, who remained there until the Germans took them away in July 1940.

There was thus no shortage of possible sources of the best available advice. Unfortunately, as it turned out, nobody really knew what was happening.

On Monday, 20th May, Ethel Wodehouse drove to the British Military hospital at Étaples, to seek advice from the Commanding Officer there, as to whether the time had now definitely come for them to flee. The Commanding Officer was so reassuring about the German advance that the Wodehouses decided not to leave until the next day. On 21st May, the Wodehouses together with their peke, Wonder, and as many of their possessions as they could pack in, set out south, towards the Somme, in their Lancia car. They possessed another car, a smaller one, and this they gave to a Miss Unger, the Swiss governness of their neighbour, Lady Furness.

Unfortunately, the Wodehouses' Lancia, which had been involved in a smash two months previously, and had, as it turned out, not been properly repaired, broke down after about two miles and had to be abandoned. The Wodehouses then returned with Miss Unger in their small car to their house. There they found a group of neighbours about to flee: Arthur Grant, his wife Ruth and daughter Jacqueline, together with an elderly acquaintance, a Mr. Lawry. The group had two vehicles: the Grants' own car, and a Ford Red Cross van belonging to another neighbour, a Mr. Kemp. They decided they would all set off together. The Wodehouses' car led the little convoy, followed by the Red Cross van, with Jacqueline Grant driving, Mr Lawry beside her; Ruth Grant was in the back of the van, with such of their belongings as they could pack in; and Arthur Grant followed in the Grants' small Simca. The plan was for them all to head for Le Treport, and if, as seemed almost certain in the congestion of fleeing refugees, they became separated, the Wodehouses were to wait for them at the next town. Unfortunately, the Ford van had hardly travelled a few hundred yards, and had just reached the junction with the main road south to the Somme, when it had broken down. What they then saw was described thus by Ruth Grant in her journal: "There was a sight we had none of us seen before – cars, carts, bicycles, every form of transport, and people walking, all in the same direction, away from Le Touquet . . . (The refugees) were carrying all they possibly could, and many cars had the family bedding strapped on the roof. It turned out handy, when they were machine-gunned from the air".

Following the break-down of the van, Jacqueline Grant took the Simca and drove to the nearby airfield, where there was a small detachment of Royal Engineers. When she asked the officer on duty if she could "borrow" two men to mend the van, the officer replied, in what seemed a parody of British attitudes: "My dear young lady, I would be glad to help, but it is totally impossible: this happens to be the mechanics' tea-time".

Eventually, however, two Royal Engineers returned with her and repaired the van.

Meanwhile, the Wodehouses had driven on as best they could through the swarms of refugees. Then, after some miles, seeing no sign of the Grants, they had stopped and waited. After a long time, and still no sign of the Grants, they had returned to look for them. By then, it was early evening, and it was decided that the best thing to do would be for them all to return home, and set out early the next day. That night, to the surprise of the Wodehouses and the Grants, there was no German bombing. The reason became clear in the morning. Opposition to the Germans had ceased that night. As Ruth Grant wrote in her journal: "Before the dew was off the rosemary bushes edging the lawn, through the green forest they rolled. First, the motorcycles, noisy, brutal and fast, then car after car in which the grey-green officers seemed to sit in tiers, all facing forward, two or three below, two or three on the folded hood".

That day, Wednesday, 22nd May 1940, the Germans occupied Le Touquet. There was no possibility thereafter for the Wodehouses to escape.

*　　*　　*

The second charge was that Wodehouse had been over-friendly with the Germans when they occupied Le Touquet, and before he was transported to the first of his internment camps.

The charge arose, at least in part, from an absurd misunderstanding of a passage in the first of Wodehouse's broadcasts, where he said: "There was scarcely an evening when two or three of them (members of the German Labour Corps) did not drop in for a bath at my house, and a beaming party on the porch afterwards."

This passage was intended to be a mildly facetious way of describing how his bath facilities were commandeered by the Germans. But instead of being taken as a joke, it was taken instead as being a straightforward statement of how Wodehouse happily entertained German soldiers.

Even George Orwell, who intended to defend Wodehouse, wrote in his essay, "In Defence of P. G. Wodehouse", already mentioned: "He (Wodehouse) was placed under house-arrest . . . German officers in the neighbourhood 'dropping in for a bath or a party'."

When Cussen interviewed him in September 1944, Wodehouse denied the charge of having welcomed and entertained the German troops, pointing out, among other things, that he did not even speak

German. But he clearly regarded the charge as so absurd, and his version so easily verifiable by Cussen interviewing fellow British residents at Le Touquet, such as their neighbours, the Grants, that he did not bother to rebut it at great length.

Cussen did indeed interview Jacqueline Grant later in 1945, and she did corroborate what Wodehouse had said.

Later still, however, Wodehouse wrote in a letter to his friend, Bill Townend, on 18th April 1953: "From Orwell's article you would think I had *invited* the blighters to come and scour their damned bodies in my bathroom. What actually happened was that at the end of the second week of occupation, the house next door became full of German Labour Corps workers, and they seemed to have got me muddled up with Tennyson's Sir Walter Vivian, the gentleman who 'all a summer's day gave his broad lawns until the set of sun up to the people'. I suppose to a man fond of German Labour Corps workers, and liking to hear them singing in his bath, the conditions would have been ideal, but they didn't suit me. I chafed, and a fat lot of good chafing did me. They came again next day and brought their friends."

Apart from unwanted visits by the soldiers, Wodehouse says in his evidence to Cussen, "we had no contact with the Germans". This, again, was confirmed to me by Jacqueline Grant.

In a rare interview which Wodehouse gave to the British magazine, Illustrated, published on 7th December 1946, the following passage occurs:

Cole (the Illustrated reporter): "A report was published that, at the time of the German occupation of Le Touquet, you were giving a cocktail party and German officers were invited as guests. The implication was that you were virtually waiting to receive them."

Wodehouse: "This idiotic story is completely untrue. I gave no cocktail party. At the time of the German occupation of Le Touquet I was fully occupied in trying to get away — first, in my own car, which broke down after going two miles, and then in a truck belonging to a neighbour, which broke down in the first hundred yards. The only German officer I ever saw at Le Touquet was the Kommandant with the glass eye, to whom British residents had to report each morning at the Paris Plage Kommandatur."

Far, indeed, from welcoming the Germans, the Wodehouses disliked and feared them. Jacqueline Grant told me that Wodehouse, during that period of the war prior to 22nd May 1940, had written several articles and draft articles and jottings which were so anti-German in tone that on the day before the Wodehouses made their two attempts to escape, Ethel Wodehouse insisted that these writings should be burned, first trying to do so in the grate and later, since the grate was not big enough, outside on the terrace of their house, Low Wood. She was afraid that if the Germans discovered them and Wodehouse were to be captured later, he would be shot out of hand. Such fears may or may not seem unfounded with hindsight: to Ethel Wodehouse and Jacqueline Grant in 1940, they were terrifyingly real.

In retrospect it is clear that the destruction of the writings, although understandable in light of the fears of Ethel Wodehouse in 1940, was a tragedy: not only was the world deprived of a substantial amount of Wodehouse's work, but Wodehouse himself was deprived of one means of proving how ridiculous were any charges that he was sympathetic to Nazism.

* * *

The next charge against Wodehouse was that he had collaborated with the Germans while he was interned, and that by this collaboration he had won for himself special comforts and privileges.

Five specific allegations against Wodehouse were collected by Cussen from persons who were interned with him at Tost. These accusations are set out in Section IV of his report, given verbatim in Appendix Eight. Summarised, the charges from each instance were that: (1) Wodehouse, it was "rumoured in the camp", had offered to go to America to write propaganda for the Germans; (ii) Wodehouse wrote to the German Foreign Service "offering his services"; (iii) Wodehouse was "notorious" among internees as being pro-German; (iv) Wodehouse "collaborated" in the camp; that he had written a "glowing" account of life in internment camps for the American press; and that he had submitted an offer to the Germans, through the "Contact Committee" at Tost, to write articles to promote better feeling between French and Germans; (v) that he had edited a pro-German weekly magazine at Tost called "The Camp".

Cussen, in his report, described all these charges as "vague", and came to disbelieve them – although positively to disprove them all was not easy. Wodehouse denied them all. That Wodehouse collaborated with the Germans during his internment is a charge which is specifically dealt with at greater length, and totally refuted below. Similarly, the overwhelming weight of the evidence discovered by Cussen and by others since, including myself, contradicts completely the charge that Wodehouse offered his services to the Germans.

Of course, it is very often, indeed usually, impossible for an innocent man to prove his innocence. That is a fact of life that is wisely embodied in the principle of English, Scottish and American law that a person is deemed innocent until proved guilty. What can be said with absolute certainty, in the case of the five charges against Wodehouse, quoted above, is that Cussen found not one jot of acceptable evidence to support any of them, and found substantial evidence to the contrary.

Before dealing with the general charge of collaboration by Wodehouse, it is instructive to consider, in more detail, the fifth specific charge above made by "a repatriated merchant seaman" – unnamed by Cussen – as an interesting, and typical, example of how large lies grow out of small misunderstandings: "It was alleged by a repatriated merchant seaman that a weekly paper called 'The Camp' (a German publication for circulation in internment camps) was edited by Wodehouse, and was pro-German in tone."

What was the truth behind this charge?

In his report, Cussen quotes Wodehouse as replying to this allegation as follows: " 'I never offered my services to the German authorities, and was never approached by them with a view to my helping them in any way. During my time at Tost, there appeared in the German-run paper, "The Camp", a very poor parody of my "Bertie Wooster" stories dealing with "Bertie" as a military man, with some such signature as "P. G. Roadhouse", though I cannot remember this exactly. I had nothing to do with this, and this should be obvious to anybody who has read the parody.' "

Not only was Wodehouse not the editor of the "The Camp", as the repatriated seaman claimed to Cussen, but he never wrote for it, and never had anything to do with it at all. The likely origin of the false statement by the merchant seaman was that there was a camp newspaper, produced by the British internees (as opposed to "The Camp" produced by the German authorities) called "Tost Times", which was of irreproachable British patriotism, of which Wodehouse was not editor, but for which he once condensed a short story of his own, already published.

The five unsubstantiated allegations against Wodehouse by fellow internees, quoted above, seem typical of the multitude of false rumours – known as "blue pigeons" or "bed-time stories" – to which Wodehouse refers, in his fifth Berlin broadcast as abounding in camp, and which "never turned out to be true".

Returning to the general charge of collaboration by Wodehouse, however, it is important to be aware that after Wodehouse was seen at Tost by the American journalist, Angus Thuermer, of Associated Press, on 26th December 1940, Thuermer wrote an article, published in the New York Times, which specifically said that Wodehouse was not receiving any special privileges from the Germans, and had indeed refused what had been offered by the Germans out of their respect for his age and reputation. This article was, of course, published before anti-Wodehouse rumours and fabrications became rife, following his release and his broadcasts from Berlin. One of the headlines in the New York Times over Thuermer's article, was actually: "He (meaning Wodehouse) Declines Favors".

Wodehouse's true attitude to his German captors was very different from that alleged in the five accusations quoted above, and it is important to understand the psychology that lay behind it. When Wodehouse was accused, in a cable sent to him after his first broadcast from Berlin, by Wesley Stout, editor of the Saturday Evening Post, of being "callous about England", Wodehouse cabled back, ". . . Cannot understand what you mean about callousness. Mine simply flippant cheerful attitude of all British prisoners. It was a point of honour with us not to whine."

An examination of the text of Wodehouse's broadcasts, combined with what is now known about the attempts by British prisoners-of-war to maintain their spirits and morale in other German camps like Colditz, confirms exactly what Wodehouse says about the "cheerful flippant attitude of all British prisoners", and the importance to them of not appearing, as a point of honour, "to whine". Such attitudes were central to Wodehouse's thinking and behaviour: by broadcasting as he did, Wodehouse believed that, in terms of the traditional British values of keeping a stiff upper lip and not complaining in adversity, he was positively behaving well, not merely that he was not behaving badly. Wodehouse wanted to show the world how a group of British internees, himself not least, could endure hardship and still keep up their spirits. This is clear from many passages in the available evidence. For example, in his statement to Cussen, Wodehouse says: ". . . I thought that people, hearing the (Berlin broadcast) talks, would admire me for having kept cheerful under difficult conditions . . ." In Wodehouse's letter to the Home Secretary, which is quoted in full later in this book, he writes that his broadcasts "were designed to show American listeners a group of Englishmen (sic) keeping up their spirits and courage under difficult conditions".

Arthur Grant's account of Wodehouse's behaviour in the four internment camps they shared was – both in letters to his wife and daughter before his release from Tost in 1944, and afterwards in conversation – clear and unambiguous: Wodehouse had never asked for special privileges from the Germans. He had never received any special privileges from them. When the Germans had offered Wodehouse a room on his own – as a gesture towards his age and international fame – he had refused to accept it, saying that he preferred sharing a dormitory with the other men. He had not collaborated with the Germans in any way whatsoever. The suggestion was ridiculous. He had been treated in every way the same as his fellow internees. He had been notably generous in sharing and lending his possessions, such as they were, with others. Like all the British internees at Tost Wodehouse had devoutly wished for, and been confident of, an ultimate British victory in the war. He had remained outwardly cheerful himself, and by his own cheerfulness had helped to maintain good morale in others. He had been popular with his fellow internees. When he was released from Tost in June 1941, none of his fellow internees, whom Grant knew, ever thought for one moment that he had "bought" his release by agreeing to do something for the Nazis: it did not occur to them: they assumed he had been released primarily because of his age, and secondly because of his international fame; they expected he would be repatriated. In short, Wodehouse had behaved impeccably.

This was told to Cussen by Grant's daughter, Jacqueline, when

Cussen interviewed her; and she subsequently told me. So completely did Cussen believe her, however, and so convinced was he, by this time, of Wodehouse's innocence, that he did not trouble to arrange an interview with Grant himself. This was understandable and perfectly proper in light of Cussen's specific task – namely, to see whether or not evidence existed to justify the prosecution of Wodehouse for treason – but it was profoundly unfortunate for Wodehouse. Had Cussen recorded in writing the evidence of Arthur Grant, Bert Haskins, and other internees who had been in a position to observe Wodehouse every day, at first hand, and had these records, together with the other evidence amassed, been made public immediately after the war by the British Government, Wodehouse's innocence could have been publicly established.

✻　　✻　　✻

The next charge against Wodehouse was that he was a Nazi sympathiser. Again, Cussen found no evidence for this. On the contrary, Jacqueline Grant described to me, as recorded earlier, how she and Ethel Wodehouse had had to burn files of his writings, in case the Germans found them, precisely because they were so anti-German in tone. Furthermore, nobody who truly knew and appreciated Wodehouse's published work could ever have believed that he was a Nazi sympathiser. Indeed, in one of the few passages in his work in any way political, there occurs the following paragraph in "The Code of the Woosters", regarding one Roderick Spode, a would-be British dictator whose followers were known as the Black Shorts. Bertie Wooster addresses him thus: ". . . It is about time that some public-spirited person came along and told you where you got off. The trouble with you, Spode, is that just because you have succeeded in inducing a handful of half-wits to disfigure the London scene by going about in black shorts, you think you're someone. You hear them shouting 'Heil, Spode!' and you imagine it is the Voice of the People. That is where you make your bloomer. What the Voice of the People is saying is: 'Look at that frightful ass Spode swanking about in footer bags! Did you ever in your puff see such a perfect perisher!' "

Nor is it conceivable that a Nazi sympathiser would have written so disrespectfully of Adolf Hitler as Wodehouse did at the beginning of his short story, "Buried Treasure": "The situation in Germany had come up for discussion in the bar parlour of the Angler's Rest, and it was generally agreed that Hitler was standing at a cross-roads and would soon have to do something definite. His present policy, said a Whisky and Splash, was mere shilly-shallying.

" 'He'll have to let it grow or shave it off' said the Whisky and Splash. 'He can't go on sitting on the fence like this. Either a man has a moustache or not. There can be no middle course.' "

On this question of any Nazi sympathies, Cussen examined in detail the journal which Wodehouse had kept in camp, and the following extract from Cussen's report is revelant:

"The Journal has been examined with a view to seeing whether Wodehouse expresses therein any sympathy with the enemy. The following entries are those which are relevant:

(i) July 31st, 1940 –
'. . . I was first to alight from train. Met old German general who asked how old I was, felt my suitcase and said it was too heavy to carry and sent for truck–asked me if I had had anything to eat or drink. Very sympathetic and kindly . . .'
(ii) August 15th –
'. . . The reason for forbidding letters is apparently that there has been a lot of sabotage at Lille, people cutting telephone wires etc., so I am told by very nice, sympathetic German lieutenant . . .'
(iii) September 8th –
'. . . The journey to Tost . . . our dear old Sergeant is with us, and the sight of him does much to take away that lost feeling. He is more like a mother than a sergeant . . .'
(iv) October 8th –
'. . . got into conversation with charming German corporal who spoke perfect English and has read all my books. Also another one had, which bucked me up enormously . . .'
(v) October 30th –
'. . . I am very fond of the two interpreters I have talked with, one grey haired (43), fresh face, veteran of last war, the other the spectacled one, who learned his English in U.S.A. (He worked for Fred Harvey hotels as newstand, and says 'Have

you got me, boys?') It bears out what I have always said that Germans are swell guys, and the only barrier between us is the one of language. I have never met an English-speaking German whom I didn't like instantly . . .'

"Having regard to the circumstances in which this journal was written (Cussen continues) I do not think any very great exception can fairly be taken even to these entries. The latter part of the entry quoted in sub-paragraph (v) above may contain sentiments with which one definitely disagrees, but Wodehouse is not the first person to have expressed such views. It must be a matter of opinion as to whether the entry in question affords an indication of the existence of a state of mind which would tend towards co-operation with the enemy."

In connection with the above extract, a number of points must be made. First, when Wodehouse was writing, he could not know of the Nazi atrocities, particularly in the concentration camps, that were later to come to light. Nor had his hatred against the Germans been intensified by experiencing the terror of bombing during the Blitz – although he had been bombed by the Germans at Le Touquet – nor by hearing Goebbels announce that Britain was to be "reduced to degradation and poverty"; nor by reading such gruesome extracts from the German press as the following passage duly reported in the British press in 1941: "Germany must tear the British empire apart bit by bit, and be influenced by not the slightest feelings of pity. Britain must be made to bleed, and every wound re-opened until she bleeds to death."

Secondly, these passages quoted above are the only ones in the whole of his camp book which are in any way remotely friendly to the Germans: there are many more passages critical of them.

Thirdly, in the words of Bill Townend, in "Performing Flea": "Plum's misfortune was that he was capable of finding things to like in the most unlikable of people, and though loathing the Nazi way of life and their lust for conquest, and their uniforms and posturings, was unwilling to associate the individual German with the excesses and crimes of his Government."

Fourthly, Wodehouse, of course, was not alone among British internees and prisoners-of-war in drawing distinctions between "good" Germans – as in the case of the sergeant above – and "bad" ones: similar distinctions are quite properly drawn by the irreproachably patriotic authors of such admired prisoner-of-war books as "The Colditz Story", and "The Wooden Horse", etc.

Fifthly, with regard to what seems the excessive tone of Wodehouse's words in section (v) of Cussens's report, quoted above, in pre-war America Wodehouse had known several German-Americans, and one of his closest friends in Hollywood was just such an English-speaking German, Raven von Barnikow. This, no doubt, coloured his feelings.

✱ ✱ ✱

The next charge against Wodehouse, which Cussen investigated, was the most serious: it was that Wodehouse had broadcast Nazi propaganda from Berlin, in much the same way as the infamous "Lord Haw Haw", and that as a result of promising to do this, he had been released from internment. Once again, Cussen found no evidence whatsoever that either part of the charge was true. Nor have I. Indeed, the exact contrary is the case.

Regarding the first part, namely that Wodehouse had broadcast Nazi propaganda, it is necessary only to read the text of the broadcasts to see that any such accusation is ludicrous. There is not a single sentence that is pro-Nazi. There is not a single sentence that is anti-British. On the contrary, Wodehouse poked fun at the Germans and specifically made clear that morale among the British internees was high.

There were five broadcasts, and each was about ten minutes long. The full text is to be found in Appendix One. Some sample sections follow here, so that the reader can judge their flavour set in the context of arguments about their significance. The opening passage of the first talk sets the tone, humorous and non-political:

"It is just possible that my listeners may seem to detect in this little talk of mine a slight goofiness, a certain disposition to ramble in my remarks. If so, the matter, as Bertie Wooster would say, is susceptible of a ready explanation. I have just emerged into the outer world after forty-nine weeks of Civil Internment in a German internment camp and the effects have not entirely worn off. I have not yet quite recovered that perfect mental balance for which in the past I was so admired by one and all.

51

"It's coming back, mind you. Look me up a couple of weeks from now, and you'll be surprised. But just at the moment I feel slightly screwy and inclined to pause at intervals in order to cut out paper dolls and stick straws in my hair – or such of my hair as I still have . . ."

The talk continued in the same tone throughout:

" . . . Since I went into business for myself as an internee, I have been in no fewer than four Ilags – some more Ilaggy than others, others less Ilaggy than some. First, they put us in a prison, then in a barracks, then in a fortress. Then they took a look at me and the rest of the boys on parade one day, and got the right idea at last. They sent us off to the local lunatic asylum at Tost in Upper Silesia, and there I have been for the last forty-two weeks . . ."

" . . . Young men, starting out in life have often asked me 'How can I become an Internee?' Well, there are several methods. My own was to buy a villa in Le Touquet on the coast of France and stay there till the Germans came along. This is probably the best and simplest system. You buy the villa and the Germans do the rest."

"At the time of their arrival, I would have been just as pleased if they had not rolled up. But they did not see it that way, and on May the twenty-second along they came, some on motor cycles, some on foot, but all evidently prepared to spend a long week-end . . ."

" . . . The proceedings were not marred by any vulgar brawling. All that happened, as far as I was concerned, was that I was strolling on the lawn with my wife one morning, when she lowered her voice and said 'Don't look now, but there comes the German army.' And there they were, a fine body of men, rather prettily dressed in green, carrying machine guns . . ."

(Readers should note that phrase, "a fine body of men". It is surely an obvious example of mild facetiousness. Yet that was one of the phrases which, Wodehouse's critics seriously and frequently asserted, demonstrated that Wodehouse was pro-German.)

" . . . One drawback to being an internee is that, when you move from spot to spot, you have to do it in company with eight hundred other men. This precludes anything in the nature of travel de luxe. We made the twenty-four hour trip in a train consisting of those 'Quarante Hommes, Huit Chevaux' things – in other words, cattle trucks. I had sometimes seen them on sidings on French railroads in times of peace, and had wondered what it would be like to be one of the Quarante Hommes. I now found out, and the answer is that it is pretty darned awful. Eight horses might manage to make themselves fairly comfortable in one of these cross-country loose-boxes, but forty men are cramped. Every time I stretched my legs, I kicked a human soul. This would not have mattered so much, but every time the human souls stretched *their* legs, they kicked *me* ..."

" ... If somebody were to ask me whose quarters I would prefer to take over, those of French convicts or Belgian soldiers, I would find it hard to say. French convicts draw pictures on the walls of their cells which bring the blush of shame to the cheek of modesty, but they are fairly tidy in their habits, whereas Belgians soldiers, as I have mentioned before, make lots of work for their successors. Without wishing to be indelicate, I may say that until you have helped to clean out a Belgian soldiers' latrine, you ain't seen nuttin'."

"It was my stay at Liège, and subsequently at the Citadel of Huy, that gave me that wholesome loathing for Belgians which is the hall-mark of the discriminating man. If I never see anything Belgian again in this world, it will be all right with me .."

(Once again, readers should be aware that Wodehouse's remarks above about the Belgians were severely criticised as showing contempt for one of the Allies and, therefore, by implication, giving a propaganda advantage to the Germans. It is also interesting that when the full texts, so-called, of the Berlin broadcasts were published by Encounter magazine in 1954, and later in the book "Performing Flea", this passage about the Belgians was removed. Other substantial changes were also made, both additions and subtractions. In general, these revisions were to make the text funnier and smoother. Nothing was changed for political reasons, as far as I could judge, unless this passage about the Belgians be counted as such. Nonetheless, it is important to note that what were previously published as Wodehouse's Berlin broadcasts were not, in fact, the true texts.)

" ... Extra parades were also called two or three times a day by the Sergeant, when there was any announcement to be made. At Tost we had a notice board, on which camp orders were posted each day, but this ingenious system had not occurred to anyone at Huy. The only way they could think of establishing communication between the front office and the internees was to call a parade. Three whistles would blow, and we would assemble in the yard, and after a long interval devoted to getting into some sort of formation we would be informed that there was a parcel for Omer – or that we must shave daily – or that we must not smoke on parade – or that we must not keep our hands in our pockets on parade – or that we might buy playing cards – (and the next day that we might not buy playing cards) – or that boys must not cluster round the guard-room trying to scrounge food from the soldiers . . ."

" . . .'Tough' is the adjective I would use to describe the whole of those five weeks at Huy. The first novelty of internment had worn off, and we had become acutely alive to the fact that we were in the soup and likely to stay there for a considerable time. Also, tobacco was beginning to run short, and our stomachs had not yet adjusted themselves to a system of rationing, which, while quite good for a prison camp, was far from being what we had been accustomed to at home. We were hearty feeders who had suddenly been put on a diet, and our stomachs sat up on their hind legs and made quite a fuss about it . . ."

" . . . An internee does not demand much in the way of bedding—give him a wisp or two of straw and he is satisfied – but at Huy it looked for a while as if there would not even be straw. However, they eventually dug us out enough to form a thin covering on the floors, but that was as far as they were able to go. Of blankets there were enough for twenty men. I was not one of the twenty. I don't know why it is, but I never am one of the twenty men who get anything. For the first three weeks, all I had over me at night was a raincoat, and one of these days I am hoping to meet Admiral Byrd and compare notes with him."

" . . .One great improvement at Tost, from my viewpoint, was that men of fifty and over were not liable for fatigues, in other words, the dirty work. At Liege and Huy there had been no age limit. We had all pitched in together, reverend elders and beardless boys alike, cleaning out latrines with one hand and peeling potatoes with the other, so to speak. At Tost, the old dodderers like myself lived the life of Riley. For us, the arduous side of life was limited to making one's bed, brushing the floor under and around it, and washing one's linen. Repairs to clothes and shoes were done in the tailor's and cobbler's shops.

"When there was man's work to be done, like hauling coal or shovelling snow, we just sat and looked on, swapping reminiscences

54

of the Victorian Age, while our juniors snapped into it. I don't know anything that so braces one up on a cold winter morning, with an Upper Silesian blizzard doing its stuff, as to light one's pipe and look out of a window and watch a gang of younger men shovelling snow. It makes you realise what the man meant who said that Age has its pleasures as well as youth . . . ."

The final talk concluded thus:

" . . . It is a curious experience, being completely shut off from the outer world, as one is in an internment camp. One lives on potatoes and rumours. One of my friends used to keep a notebook in which he would jot down all the rumours that spread through the corridors, and they made curious reading. To military prisoners, I believe, rumours are known for some reason as 'Blue Pigeons'. We used to call them bedtime stories. They never turned out to be true, but a rumour a day kept depression away, so they served their purpose. Certainly, whether owing to bedtime stories or simply the feeling that, if one was in, one was in and it was no use making heavy weather about it, the morale of the men at Tost was wonderful. I never met a more cheerful crowd, and I loved them like brothers."

"With this talk, I bring to an end the story of my adventures as British Civilian Prisoner Number 796, and before concluding I should like once more to thank all the kind people in America who wrote me letters while I was in camp. Nobody who has not been in a prison camp can realise what letters, especially letters like those I received, mean to an internee . . . ."

These extracts are typical of the talks as a whole, and make clear that any charge that they were Nazi propaganda, or that Wodehouse was a kind of "Lord Haw-Haw", were ridiculously false.

*　　*　　*

However, it was not just Wodehouse's broadcasts on German radio that enraged large sections of the British public, and dismayed Americans. Even worse, as far as the actual words Wodehouse used were concerned, was the interview on 26th June 1941 given by Wodehouse to the American correspondent in Berlin for the Columbia Broadcasting System, Harry W. Flannery. (The United States was, of course, still neutral at that date.) In this interview, which lasted only 3½ minutes, of which some 50 seconds were taken up with Flannery describing what Wodehouse looked like, Wodehouse was heard saying four things at which great offence was taken in the United Kingdom, and to a lesser extent in the United States.

The first remark by Wodehouse was: "... I'm living here at the Adlon (Hotel in Berlin) – have a suite on the third floor, a very nice one, too – and I come and go as I please..."

The second remark was:

Flannery: "Do you mind being a prisoner-of-war in this fashion, Mr. Wodehouse?"

Wodehouse: "Not a bit. As long as I have a typewriter and plenty of paper and a room to work in, I'm fine."

The third remark was made in the context of the writing Wodehouse had been doing while in internment camp: "... But I'll tell you something about the war and my work which has been bothering me a good deal. I'm wondering whether the kind of people and the kind of England I write about, will live after the war – whether England wins or not, I mean" (The key phrase there was "... whether England wins or not...".)

Fourthly, and particularly grating to British ears, were Wodehouse's comments about America, remembering that Wodehouse was a British subject:

Flannery: "Anything you'd like to say, Mr. Wodehouse, about the United States?"

Wodehouse: "Yes, I'd like to be back there again. You see, I've always thought of the United States as sort of my country – lived there almost all the time since 1909 – and I long to get back there once more. But I guess there's nothing I can do about that now, except write stories for you people. I hope you continue to like them. Well, goodnight, everybody."

These four passages from the C.B.S. interview were taken to show that Wodehouse was living in freedom, and almost luxury, in the enemy capital; that he was perfectly content to do so, and had probably purchased his ability to do so by agreeing to collaborate with the Nazis; that he was defeatist about the British winning the war; and that he had no desire to share the privations and miseries and dangers of his own native land in time of war. In short, that his words in this interview showed him to be cowardly, treacherous and unpatriotic.

What was the truth? The truth was none of these things. What actually happened was that Flannery, who was strongly anti-Nazi, disliked and despised Wodehouse, because he believed that in fact Wodehouse was half-dupe and half-collaborator, and he wanted this to be evident from the interview. Flannery actually says in his book, "Assignment to Berlin", published in 1942, that Wodehouse allowed himself to be "bought" and that he agreed to make uncensored broadcasts in return for his freedom from the internment camp. Flannery wrote: "By this time the Wodehouse plot was evident. It was one of the best Nazi publicity stunts of the war, the first with a human angle. That was because it was not the work of Dr. Goebbels, but of Hollywood-wise Plack instead. (Werner Plack was a German actor who had returned from the United States to work for the German Foreign Office. His role in the Wodehouse affair is discussed in greater detail later in this book.) Plack had gone to the camp near Gleiwitz (Tost) to see Wodehouse, found that the author was completely without political sense, and had an idea. He suggested to Wodehouse that in return for being released from the prison camp he write a series of broadcasts about his experiences; there would be no censorship and he would put them on the air himself. In making that proposal Plack showed that he knew his man. He knew that Wodehouse made fun of the English in all his stories and that he seldom wrote in any other way, that he was still living in the period about which he wrote and had no conception of Nazism and all it meant. Wodehouse was his own Bertie Wooster.

"Plack knew that the stories would tell some unpleasant truths about the Nazis, but that they would all be lightened by the Wodehouse wit. He knew that Wodehouse would not be dangerously critical; he never was. He could be trusted to write an uncensored script, and since he was Wodehouse he would gain an audience for the Nazi programmes. Thus people might be lured into hearing the general Nazi propaganda line, but even if they heard no more than Wodehouse, some of the criticism of the Nazis would be averted by Wodehouse himself. . . ."

Flannery was entirely wrong in his belief that Werner Plack had visited Wodehouse at Tost, and that he was the originator of the broadcasting plan. The infinitely more complex reality of what happened is set out later in this book. Flannery clearly disliked Plack, but Plack, who had known the Wodehouses slightly in Hollywood before the war, proved a good friend to them: Plack protected Wodehouse, whom he liked and admired, and whom he realised was not a Nazi sympathiser or collaborator, from the clutches of Goebbels' Ministry of Propoganda; he saw to it that Wodehouse was able to get on with his writing in peace; to amuse the Wodehouses, he once walked with them through the streets of Berlin dressed in a British army uniform he had picked up at Tobruk, wearing a helmet on which its former British owner had inscribed "Down with Hitler!"; he once commandeered a Gestapo car and drove 60 kilometres to take some birdseed to a parrot that Ethel Wodehouse had left behind in France, and about which she was worried; and, most importantly, he prevented the Gestapo from forcibly taking Wodehouse back to Germany when the Germans evacuated Paris in August 1944. An indication that the Wodehouses realised that Plack had been a good friend to them was that Ethel became god-mother to his son in 1948.

But to return to the damaging words spoken by Wodehouse in the interview, Flannery himself, in fact, wrote every word beforehand, including those spoken by Wodehouse, after a meeting the day before with him. When, on the programme, listeners thought they heard Flannery and Wodehouse asking and answering spontaneous questions this was not so. Flannery and Wodehouse were reading word for word from a carefully prepared script.

In the interview with the British journalist, Hubert Cole, in the issue of Illustrated magazine of 7th December 1946, already mentioned, there occurs the following passage:

Cole: "The phrase which has been singled out in your talks as being defeatist and pro-Nazi is 'whether England wins the war (sic) or not'. Why did you include this in your script?"

Wodehouse: "I didn't. There is no such phrase in my talks. It occurred in a brief interview with me by the American representative of the Columbia Broadcasting System in Berlin. He wrote the entire script, including the words you mention, and I read them without realising their intention. I did not even notice them at the time."

In his interview with Flannery, Wodehouse was not giving evidence that he was cowardly, treacherous and unpatriotic, but he was certainly demonstrating that he was too trusting, too unsuspicious, too amiable, and too innocent. Flannery realised the effect which Wodehouse's words, scripted by Flannery, would have on the world. Wodehouse did not. When Flannery wrote the words about Wodehouse's "very nice" suite at the Adlon, and how he, Wodehouse, had put up with his role as "prisoner-of-war", Wodehouse thought that he was creditably making light of his experience; he thought people would admire him for not complaining. He was wrong. Flannery manipulated him, and took advantage of Wodehouse's excessively unsuspecting and amiable nature.

As regards his remarks about his feelings for America, he allowed Flannery to get him to say, in an excess of amiability, things not only pleasing to his American listeners – Wodehouse was indeed deeply grateful to all the Americans, over one hundred, who had written to him while he was at Tost internment camp – but things which were factually incorrect. Wodehouse had not lived "almost all that time" in America since 1909. Furthermore, Wodehouse himself in a letter to Townend in 1946, rebuked George Orwell for saying much the same in his essay "In Defence of P. G. Wodehouse". Wodehouse wrote:

"I wish these critics wouldn't distort facts in order to make a point. George Orwell calls my stuff Edwardian (which God knows it is. No argument about that, George) and says the reason for it being Edwardian is that I did not set foot in England for sixteen years and so lost touch with conditions there. Sixteen years, mark you, during most of which I was living in London and was known as Beau Wodehouse of Norfolk Street." And, of course, Wodehouse had lived at Le Touquet since 1934, except for twelve months in Hollywood.

The damage which this interview on C.B.S. did to Wodehouse, arose not merely from his own words, although it was these that caused by far the greatest damage to his reputation. Flannery's words also were damaging. In his introduction to the interview, Flannery described to his listeners what Wodehouse looked like: ". . . a tall, slender man of 60, with sparse straggly grey hair around a bald pate, brown tortoise-shell glasses resting on a fair-sized nose, with a wide smile over a square chin . . ." He then went on to describe what clothes he was wearing, finishing up by remarking: "Looks rather colourful."

No criticism that was provable could be read into this comment, yet somehow the impression is left with the listener that Wodehouse should not have been "colourful" in the circumstances. Even the "wide smile" is made to seem inappropriate.

Furthermore, after Flannery had finished, and returned listeners to New York, the C.B.S. link-man and presenter in New York, Elmer

Davis, made the following comment: "Mr. Wodehouse's many friends in the United States will be glad to know that he is free and that he is apparently comfortable and happy. Mr. Wodehouse seems to be more fortunate than most of the other Englishmen in his internment camp, whose release would perhaps have had less publicity value for the Germans, and, of course, he was only in an internment camp to begin with, which is a very different thing from a concentration camp. People who get out of concentration camps, such as Dachau, for instance – well, in the first place, not a great many of them get out, and, when they do, they are seldom able to broadcast."

This comment by Davis in New York was certainly intended to be unfriendly to Wodehouse, and was widely taken as such. The New York Times on 11th July 1941 said that Davis believed Wodehouse's phrase ". . . whether England wins (the war) or not" was "subtle appeasement propaganda". Davis' tone of voice, as well as the words, reinforced a belief in the listeners that somehow Wodehouse had received improperly preferential treatment. While not untrue, it was misleading to stress that Wodehouse seemed to have been "more fortunate than other Englishmen in his internment camp". It was, as has been noted earlier, the German custom, from 1939 until late 1942, to let all internees out of camp when they reached the age of 60. Several of those interned with Wodehouse had in fact been so released. In a letter to Townend in May 1942, from Berlin, Wodehouse wrote: "I was released because I was on the verge of sixty. When I was in Loos prison the first week, a dozen of our crowd were released because they were sixty, including my cell-mate, William Cartmell, the Étaples piano tuner. Of course, he may have made a bargain with the German Government, offering, if set free, to tune its piano half-price, but I don't think so. It all looked pretty genuine to me."

Although Wodehouse, by his uncritical attitude towards what Flannery had written for him, must take some blame for the vilification that was heaped on him, in all that was written and spoken about his own Berlin broadcasts, Wodehouse suffered greatly and unfairly from mis-statements, misunderstandings and deliberate distortions. His own broadcasts were confused with the Flannery interview; the Flannery radio interview was confused with other non-radio interviews he gave to newspapers and magazine journalists; those interviews were confused with the article he had written for the Saturday Evening Post while he was still in the Tost internment camp, "My War with Germany". Flannery's book, "Assignment to Berlin", contains extensive passages of purported fact which I found to be false, such as the claim that Plack visited Wodehouse at Tost and persuaded him to broadcast in return for his freedom. Not only did Plack himself assure me that this was completely untrue, but he also said that almost everything Flannery wrote about Wodehouse was either pure invention, absurd exaggeration, or else that he had simply drawn wrong conclusions from what he had heard or seen. According to Wodehouse himself much of what Flannery wrote about him was simply invented. In a letter to Townend he wrote: "Did you see a book called – I forget what, but something by Harry Flannery, one of the American correspondents in Berlin? If so, I hope you didn't believe this bilge he wrote about me . . . All the talks he reports as taking place between him and me are pure invention. I only saw him twice, but from his book you would think we were always together. I wish, by the way, when people invent conversations with me, they wouldn't give me such rotten dialogue . . ."

Wodehouse suffered considerably from journalists inventing or misunderstanding events and words. An instructive example of this kind of misunderstanding, plus heavily imaginative embroidery, was when Wodehouse was quoted as saying, in an interview given to an American correspondent in Berlin in 1941, that he could never feel "belligerent" about another country. This was taken to mean that Wodehouse was unpatriotic, and therefore lent further credence to the belief that he was some kind of Nazi collaborator. What Wodehouse had actually said and meant was far different, as he explained in a letter to Townend in 1953: "Writers on daily and weekly papers always will go all out for the picturesque. When they interview you, they invariably alter and embroider.

"As a rule, this does not matter much. If on your arrival in New York you are asked 'What do you think of our high buildings?' and you reply, 'I think your high buildings are wonderful', and it comes out as 'I think your high buildings are wonderful. I should like to see some of these income-tax guys jump off the top of them', no harm is done. The sentiment pleases the general public, and even the officials of the Internal Revenue Department probably smile indulgently, as men who know that they are going to have the last laugh. But when a war is in progress, it is kinder to the interviewee not to indulge the imagination.

"When I arrived in Berlin, I told an interviewee that I had found it difficult to be belligerent in camp, a mild pleasantry by which I intended to convey the feeling of helplessness – of having to be just a number and a well-behaved number at that, which comes over you when you find yourself on the wrong side of the barbed wire. But it did not get over. It was too subtle. The interviewer sniffed at it, patted it with his paws, wrinkled his forehead over it. Then he thought he saw what I was driving at, and penned the following:

" 'I have never been able to work up a belligerent feeling,' said Mr. Wodehouse. 'Just as I am about to feel belligerent about some country, I meet some nice fellow from it and lose my belligerency.' (Have you ever heard me talk like that?) With the result that I was accused of expressing unpatriotic sentiments and being indifferent to the outcome of the war."

It must also be said that in various accounts which Wodehouse gave to different people at different times, there are certain small inaccuracies and apparent discrepancies. For example, readers will note that in his letter to the Home Secretary from Paris in 1944, he says that he himself first proposed that he broadcast; in his letter to R. T. Rees in The Alleynian magazine (quoted later in this book) he says that a German friend suggested the idea to him. Such a discrepancy, and others which readers will note in evidence quoted in this book, does not invalidate the essential truth of Wodehouse's account, and is entirely attributable to the difficulties of remembering precise details long after they happened, and of expressing complexities with the succinctness that a specific occasion may require.

*   *   *

There remained, however, the serious charge that Wodehouse had bought his freedom from Tost by agreeing to broadcast. The strange and complicated truth about the reasons for Wodehouse's release from internment camp, and subsequent broadcasts from Berlin, was as follows:

In 1940, the head of the private office of the German Foreign

Minister, Ribbentrop, was one Dr. Paul Schmidt. Soon after Wode-houses's capture at Le Touquet in May 1940, there began to arrive on Schmidt's desk frequent appeals to have Wodehouse released, or to have him exchanged for a German national interned by the British. These appeals came from a number of sources. First, there was an important and well-publicised petition organised in the United States and presented to the German Embassy in Washington by the United States Senator, W. Warren Barbour. It asked that Wode-house be returned to the United States, which was then, of course, still neutral. This was, incidentally, a somewhat curious request as Wodehouse was a British, not an American, citizen. Nonetheless, it elicited a sympathetic response from the German Chargé d'Affaires in Washington, Dr. Hans Thomsen. He wrote to Barbour on 9 July 1940: "You may rest assured that the American friends of Mr. Wodehouse who transmitted this petition through your good offices need not feel any anxiety about his fate as far as the German authorities are concerned. As to the possibility of Mr. Wodehouse's return to the United States of America is concerned, I think this is a matter which the American Red Cross ought to be able to expedite."

Senator Barbour, however, and his co-signatories were not the only persons badgering the German authorities to have Wodehouse released. Others included his American agent, Paul Reynolds, who had Wodehouse as his only – and very lucrative – client: he was desperately eager, therefore, to have Wodehouse released.

In addition, American newspaper correspondents in Paris, such as Dorothy Bess of the Saturday Evening Post, had also been making approaches to various German departments to have Wodehouse freed. In evidence to Cussen, Dorothy Bess said: "Towards the latter part of August, or in early September 1940, I heard from the Ameri-can Consul at Lille that Mrs. P. G. Wodehouse was living in that city or nearby and that she was worried about her husband and was in financial difficulties.

"As Mr. Wodehouse was a writer for the Post I was naturally interested. My husband was making arrangements to go to Berlin, and I thought we might be able to find out where he was and perhaps arrange his release.

"From then on I tried to obtain the release of Mr. Wodehouse.

"We approached the Foreign Office, the Propaganda Ministry

·and the Gestapo. Each said that he was in military custody and that they could do nothing . . .

"To my knowledge both American and German organisations and individuals were also making efforts to secure the release of Mr. Wodehouse . . ."

Among the German representations was one from a certain Baron Raven von Barnikow. Von Barnikow was a major in the German Air Force. During the First World War he had been a member of the famous Richthofen squadron. Following the war, he had emigrated to the United States, and had become a stockbroker. In 1929, he had met the Wodehouses in New York, and had later become a close friend. Unknown to Wodehouse, von Barnikow had been trying to have him returned to the United Kingdom, in exchange for a German manufacturer of screws, then interned there.

The next factors in the tangled series of events which led to Wodehouse's release concerned the position of the German Foreign Office. Put succinctly, these were as follows: first, one of the most crucial aims of the German Foreign Office at that time was to keep the United States out of the war. Secondly, Schmidt, as head of Ribbentrop's private office, was strongly conscious of the need to achieve some striking success in order to increase the influence of the Foreign Office in Nazi circles. Thirdly, there was an intense rivalry between Ribbentrop's Foreign Office and Goebbels' Ministry of Propaganda: the Foreign Office considered itself as experienced and civilised, and Goebbels' colleagues as uncouth and narrow-minded. Fourthly, it was then the custom in Germany, and in German-occupied territories, as already mentioned, to release internees when they reached the age of sixty.

Schmidt put these factors together, and evolved the following plan: he would arrange for a well-publicised release of Wodehouse, which would please Senator Barbour and the other American signatories of petitions about Wodehouse, flatter American public opinion generally that American wishes were taken seriously by the German Government, and thus help consolidate American neutralist feeling. At the same time, it would demonstrate the professional expertise of the Foreign Office not only in its own field of foreign relations, but also in the field of propaganda – which would be a gratifying victory over Goebbels' Ministry of Propaganda. Furthermore, it would mean hardly any stretching of the rules covering internees, as Wodehouse's sixtieth birthday was on 15 October 1941, and he was therefore due to be released soon anyway.

It is important to understand that the value of Wodehouse to Schmidt was precisely that he was *not* a Nazi sympathiser nor a collaborator. Had he been a Nazi sympathiser, there would have been little remarkable about his release. For Schmidt's purpose of reinforcing American neutralist opinion to be achieved, it was essential that Wodehouse be seen to be released because of American pressure.

Such, then, was Schmidt's original plan. However, it ran into a formidable snag: the Gestapo refused to sanction Wodehouse's release.

While matters thus remained in deadlock because of the Gestapo refusal to sanction the release, a further factor in the case was introduced by another Paul Schmidt. This Schmidt, who had been an English language interpreter for Hitler, was now head of the Foreign Office department that dealt with relations with the American press, which was the department where Plack worked. Schmidt, as it happened, was an admirer of Wodehouse's work, although he had never met him. He had read the article, "My War with Germany", which Wodehouse had written in internment in 1940 – parts of which have been quoted earlier in this book – and suggested to the other Schmidt that Wodehouse might be interested in broadcasting an account of his experiences in the same light-hearted vein.

The other Schmidt thought this an excellent idea, since, if Wodehouse were to agree, it would dramatise the fact of his release, and thus increase its impact on American opinion. The Gestapo then agreed to withdraw their objections.

At this point, three matters must be emphasised. First, it never occurred to anybody closely involved at this stage – neither to the Schmidts, Werner Plack, or the Gestapo – that Wodehouse would broadcast anything that could be thought of as Nazi propaganda. Such a thing, even if it had been remotely likely, which it was not, would have completely vitiated the purpose of the exercise. Secondly, it was agreed that Wodehouse was not to be asked directly at this stage if he would broadcast when he was released, as any apparently conditional link between his release and his agreement to

65

broadcast would again vitiate the purpose of the exercise. Wode-house was to be sounded out discreetly; that is, without knowing the full background: if he raised no objection to broadcasting, good. If he declined, equally he would be released. Thirdly, none of the Germans believed that, in asking Wodehouse to broadcast, they were asking him to do anything remotely dishonourable. Plack told me that it never even occurred to them that Wodehouse would be attacked by the British or Americans for broadcasting to America the same kind of material which he had already had published in the American press.

Following agreement with the Gestapo, the Foreign Office asked the Lagerführer at Tost, Oberleutnant Buchelt, to discover Wode-house's attitude to the general idea of broadcasting. Buchelt therefore summoned Wodehouse to his office in May 1941.

When Wodehouse arrived in the office, Buchelt made reference to Wodehouse's light-hearted article, "My War with Germany". Wodehouse described what happened next in his statement to Cussen: "The Lagerführer told me how much he had enjoyed the article and then said, 'Why don't you do some broadcasts on similar lines for your American readers?' I said, 'I should love to', or 'There's nothing I should like better', or some similar phrase. These remarks were quite casual and made no impression on my mind. . . . The inference I draw from this episode is either (a) that he had been told to sound me out as to my willingness to broadcast, or (b) that having been informed by me that I was willing – as I have described above – he reported to Berlin."

There was, however, an even further complication then introduced. This was the role played by Goebbels' Ministry of Propaganda. As has been mentioned already, there existed a strong rivalry and dislike between Ribbentrop's and Goebbels' ministries. Until Wodehouse had actually been released, the Ministry of Propaganda knew little about the Wodehouse case. But after Wodehouse's interview with Flannery, and after the first of Wodehouse's own broadcasts, the Ministry of Propaganda realised, from some of the reactions, such as those of Flannery himself and Elmer Davis of CBS in New York, that Wodehouse's release and broadcasts could be distorted to achieve a different aim from that of the Foreign Office.

The Ministry of Propaganda decided that greater advantage to Germany could be achieved by presenting Wodehouse as a man who had made the broadcasts because he was a Nazi sympathiser, a kind of second Lord Haw-Haw. To achieve this, they acquired Wodehouse's broadcasts from the German radio authorities, without the knowledge or permission of the Foreign Office. The Ministry of Propaganda then arranged for these broadcasts to be transmitted again, this time to the United Kingdom, and sedulously fostered the notion among the neutral journalists in Berlin that Wodehouse was a Nazi collaborator and sympathiser. But even before learning of the activities of the Ministry of Propaganda, Schmidt – that is, the Schmidt who was head of the department that looked after American press relations – gave Plack specific instructions that he was to make certain that Wodehouse and William Joyce (Lord Haw-Haw) never met. Schmidt had never intended to make Wodehouse look a traitor; knew that in fact he was not a traitor; and after the first misunderstandings from the United States and United Kingdom, took trouble to try to ensure that he was not thought to be a traitor. As a further example of this concern, Schmidt told Plack to do his best to ensure that Wodehouse was able to pursue his normal writing habits, so that he, Wodehouse, could legitimately – as Schmidt conceived it – support himself without receiving any financial help from the German Government in case this made him look like a collaborator.

There is, however, one small mystery unsolved. In his testimony to Cussen, Wodehouse says that he foolishly and unthinkingly accepted 250 marks – worth, at that time, some £22 – from Plack as payment for his broadcasts. When I mentioned this to Plack, he was very surprised. He said that he could not recall having given Wodehouse any money; said that such a sum would have been absurdly small, by commercial standards, had it been decided to pay Wodehouse; but that, in any case, it had been Schmidt's specific policy that Wodehouse should not be paid anything by the German Government. Plack could not think what money Wodehouse could have been referring to, and said whatever it was, it was not payment.

The Ministry of Propaganda, however, not content with trying to distort the significance of the broadcasts which Wodehouse had already made, intended to try to use Wodehouse for broadcasting in the future. They did in fact ask him in May 1943 to fly to Katyn, where the Germans had just discovered the graves of 4,000 Polish soldiers massacred by Soviet forces, so that he could broadcast on the subject. Wodehouse angrily refused, made an official complaint to the Foreign Office through Plack, and said he would rather return to an internment camp for the duration of the war than make any further broadcasts on any subject whatsoever.

From evidence in Gestapo files, revealed in a submission written for Cussen by an Austrian national, Freddie Kraus in 1945, and quoted later in this book, it appears that the Ministry of Propaganda was under a grotesque illusion about Wodehouse's place in the literary world: the Ministry of Propaganda thought that Wodehouse was a modern Goethe. It was this view that led the Ministry of Propaganda, at first, to place such importance in making Wodehouse appear to be a Nazi sympathiser.

To sum up, Plack made it clear to me beyond doubt that Wodehouse did not "buy" his release by agreeing to broadcast; had never been visited by Plack at Tost; did not even know he was going to be released until the day it happened; received no special favours whatsoever from the German Government either in camp or after his release; and at no time, to Plack's knowledge, ever knowingly said or did anything anti-British, anti-American or pro-Nazi. The charge that Wodehouse was a Nazi sympathiser was ludicrously false.

Turning from theory and intention to what actually happened, the circumstances of Wodehouse's release were as follows: He was summoned from playing in a camp cricket match on the evening of 21st June 1941, when, to his complete surprise, he was told to pack his bags at once, refused permission to take the half-finished manuscript of his novel "Money in the Bank" with him, and was taken overnight by train to Berlin, with one other British internee. Arriving in Berlin before seven o'clock the next morning, Sunday, 22nd June 1941, Wodehouse, the other internee, and their two guards in plain clothes, tried several hotels which were all full, before finding suitable accommodation at the Adlon.

At the Adlon Hotel, Wodehouse met his old Hollywood friend, Raven von Barnikow. Von Barnikow told Wodehouse he had been informed of his release by their mutual Hollywood acquaintance, Werner Plack, who was now in the German Foreign Office. Von Barnikow also told Wodehouse that his, von Barnikow's, cousin, the

Baroness von Bodenhausen, to whom he was engaged, would be glad to have Wodehouse stay at her house, Degenershausen, some seventeen miles from Magdeburg, in the Harz mountains. Von Barnikow then said he would go back to his own hotel, the Bristol, and get Wodehouse some clothes, as Wodehouse had nothing but the suit he was wearing. As they were walking through the lobby of the Adlon, they ran into Plack.

Wodehouse described the next crucial events thus: "He (Plack) asked me if I was tired after my journey and how I liked Camp. It was in the course of this conversation that I mentioned the number of letters I'd received from American readers, and and said it was maddening not being able to answer them. Von Barnikow then went off to get the clothes, and Plack asked me if I would like to broadcast to America. I said 'Yes', and he said he would have me brought to his office next day to arrange details. He then hurried off. Shortly after this, before lunch, I met Lager Führer Buchelt in the lobby. He was in civilian clothes. He congratulated me on being released, and I told him I was broadcasting my experiences. He made no reference to our previous conversation. . . On the following morning, 23rd June, I was taken by the plain-clothes men to Plack's office in the Foreign Office, where he explained the method of making wax discs . . . On Wednesday, 25th June, I think I must have written and recorded my first talk. . . As regards the making of the record for the first broadcast, I wrote it on the typewriter, which Mrs. Bess, an American journalist, had by now sent me, and handed it to Werner Plack at the Adlon. I was driven with Plack to the broadcasting place where the manuscript was censored by three officials. . . and I then spoke it into the device, the actual recording taking place in an adjoining room."

On Friday, 27th June, Wodehouse went with Baroness von Bodenhausen to the Harz mountains, and with the exception of two visits to Berlin to record the four further talks, stayed there until November. He did no other work of any kind whatsoever for the German authorities. He was asked, as has been mentioned above, but he refused.

When Wodehouse realised his broadcasts had been misunderstood, he was deeply distressed. He suffered, as he said to Cussen in his evidence, "a great deal of mental pain". On at least three separate occasions, with three separate plans, he pleaded with the Germans to allow him to return to the United Kingdom to explain his innocence. He first proposed travelling by train through Eastern Europe and Turkey to Palestine, and thence back to London. This request was refused: the Ministry of Propaganda – as opposed to the Foreign Office – saw still too much potential propaganda material in Wodehouse. Secondly, he applied to return to London by way of neutral Lisbon. Again he was refused. Since he was not allowed to return himself to the United Kingdom to explain the truth, on 21st November 1942, Wodehouse wrote a letter to the British Foreign Office, through the offices of the neutral Swiss embassy in Berlin, proclaiming his innocent intentions in broadcasting, and his continuing loyalty to King George VI. This letter read as follows:

"Sir – In the hope that by doing so I shall be able to re-establish myself in the eyes of the British Government and people and to remove the bad impression created by my unfortunate broadcasts over the German short wave system in July 1941, may I be allowed to put before you the circumstances connected with these. I am not attempting to minimise my blunder, which I realise was inexcusable, but I feel that I can place certain facts before His Majesty's Government which will show that I was guilty of nothing more than a blunder.

"In the press and on the radio of Great Britain it has been stated that I bought my release from internment by making a bargain with the German Government, whereby they on their side were to set me free and I on mine undertook to broadcast German propaganda to the United States.

"This I can emphatically deny. I was released, as were all internees who had reached that age, because I was 60 years old. In the first week of my internment, at Loos Prison, a dozen men were sent home because they were 60 or over. I left the camp a year later in company with another internee of that age, who was released at the same time and for the same reason. I mention this to show that no special consideration was extended to me, and that there was never any suggestion at any time that the German Government were expecting a quid pro quo.

"Nor did the suggestion that I should broadcast come from the German Government. It happened that the first man I met on arriving in Berlin was an old Hollywood friend of mine, who had returned to Germany at the beginning of the war to work in the Foreign Office. And after we had talked for a while and the conversation had turned to my plans for the future, I said that the thing I was anxious to do as soon as possible was to make a few broadcasts to the United States, to let my correspondents there know how I had been getting along.

"In the last 30 weeks of my captivity, I should mention, I had received a great number of letters from American readers of my books, full of sympathy and kindness and all very curious for details of the life I was living, and none of these had I been able to answer. For in camp internees are allowed to write only to near relatives.

"These letters had been preying on my mind. I felt that their writers, having no means to knowing the circumstances, must be thinking me ungrateful and ungracious in ignoring them. I still could not reply to them individually, but I thought that if I were to speak on the radio, describing my adventures, it would at least be a sort of interim acknowledgement. Next day I arranged to do five talks, covering the five phases of my imprisonment – the start at Le Touquet; the first week in Loos Prison; the second week in Liége Barracks; the third, fourth, fifth, sixth and seventh weeks at the Citadel of Huy; and the last forty-two weeks in Tost Lunatic Asylum.

"I can now, of course, see that this was an insane thing to do, and I regret it sincerely. My only excuse is that I was in an emotional frame of mind, and the desire to make some return for all those letters had become an obsession, causing me to overlook the enormity of my action.

"It seemed to me at the time that there could be no harm in reading over the radio a short series of purely humorous and frivolous reminiscences which, if I had been in England, would have appeared in Punch. I had written these talks while in camp and had read them to an audience of fellow-internees, who were amused by them, which would not have been the case had they contained the slightest suggestion of German propaganda.

"All this, I realise, does not condone the fact that I used the

71

German short wave system as a means of communication with my American public, but I hope that it puts my conduct in a better light.

"With regard to my life since I left camp, I have been living during the Spring, Summer and Autumn at the home of the family of another Hollywood friend. In the Winter, when the house is closed, I have been obliged to stay at the Adlon Hotel, as I do not speak German and the difficulties in the way of living anywhere else would have been insuperable. All my expenses are paid by myself, partly with borrowed money and partly from the proceeds of the sale of my wife's jewellery. If the impression in England is that I am being maintained by the German Government, I should like to deny it totally.

"I should like to conclude by expressing my sincere regret that a well-meant but ill-considered action on my part should have given the impression that I am anything but a loyal subject of His Majesty.

I am, Sir, your obedient servant,
(Signed) P. G. Wodehouse."

The third occasion when Wodehouse tried to leave Germany was when, in April 1943, Wodehouse sought permission to go to neutral Sweden. Again, he was refused.

*　　*　　*

The final charge against Wodehouse was that he had lived in comfort, and indeed luxury, particularly while staying at the Adlon Hotel in Berlin, at the expense of the German Government. This was almost universally believed during the war, as has been shown from quotations already given from the British, American and Swedish press.

In fact, both parts of the charge were totally false. Wodehouse lived a simple life – he spent most of the day working at his books, or walking – and paid for everything himself. Details of his finances are given in the appendices. The Wodehouses lived at the Adlon, when they did so, because they were required by the Germans to live there. The restricted style of their living can be gathered from a detail told to me by Plack: if ever there was any bread left on the Wodehouses' table at the end of a meal, they took it with them to their room to eat later.

In his report written in September 1944, Cussen wrote that he expected later to discover evidence that the Wodehouses, and in particular Ethel, whose personality he described as "flamboyant", had behaved improperly towards the Germans. In this he was wrong.

While the Wodehouses lived in Berlin, Werner Plack saw them regularly and frequently. When they moved to Paris, in September 1943, he saw them less frequently, but still regularly. Plack told me that within his knowledge, at no time, neither in Berlin nor Paris, did the Wodehouses play the "prominent part in social life" ascribed to them in sections of the press. They never went to social gatherings in public at all. Neither of them spoke German. In Berlin they never on any occasion entertained anyone at their hotel. They had almost nothing to do with German officialdom other than with Plack, part of whose job, as a member of the Foreign Office, was to keep an eye on them. The Wodehouses never went to the theatre, opera or cinema. Occasionally, they would go for a meal with Plack in his flat, or with others of their small circle of acquaintances, such as Frau von Wulfing, an Englishwoman married to a German. According to Plack, nothing whatsoever that the Wodehouses did could have been construed by the British as behaving improperly to the enemy. In a social sense, their lives were extremely quiet.

But in another sense, Ethel Wodehouse – though not Plum – was not quiet but extremely noisy. It was a misunderstanding of the sense in which she was noisy that at first led Cussen to believe that she had been overly friendly with the Germans. Ethel Wodehouse simply talked loudly and a lot. Every time she entered a room was an occasion. She was indeed "flamboyant". She was the kind of woman who was never embarrassed to make a great fuss if matters were not ordered as she wished. But although Ethel was personally noisy, the pattern of her life, as of her husband's, was very quiet.

Two incidents described to me by Plack illustrate well this flamboyant side of Ethel Wodehouse's character. On one occasion, Plack arrived in the dining-room of the Adlon where the Wodehouses were having lunch. (They were, it must be emphasised, required by the German authorities to stay there.) Immediately, Ethel Wodehouse summoned him to their table in a piercing voice: "Werner, will you

73

please tell the head waiter that I have been waiting to be served for an hour and a half! An hour and a half! What's more, this table wobbles!" Whereupon she took a white bread roll – rationed and rare – from the table and jammed it under one of the legs to keep the table steady. According to Plack, the Germans in the dining-room could hardly believe their ears and eyes: first, the loud and angry voice speaking in English, and then the almost sacrilegious treatment of the roll.

Another incident that illustrates Ethel Wodehouse's flamboyant character was as follows: one day, Plack was standing in the lobby of the Adlon. A man in the uniform of a naval officer was telling the hotel receptionist that he was there on behalf of Admiral Doenitz, the head of the German Navy. Doenitz would be arriving the next day and would require two rooms: in one of them he would be keeping his pet Alsatian dog. The receptionist threw up his hands in horror: it was not possible to have a dog in the hotel: it was against the rules which were strictly kept. But, the naval officer said, this was for the great Admiral Doenitz.

The receptionist said it made no difference. The naval officer persisted. A heated argument followed. While this argument was in progress, Ethel Wodehouse appeared, walking down the main staircase with her Pekinese, Wonder, on a lead. The naval officer pointed out furiously that apparently dogs were allowed in the Adlon. "Ah, well, yes," replied the receptionist, "but you must understand that that is Mrs. Wodehouse." Doenitz was not allowed to bring his dog.

Ethel Wodehouse had managed to persuade the hotel to allow her to keep her dog there, not by the intervention of any German official, but because she had insisted, at great length and volume of decibels, until she got her way.

Such was Ethel Wodehouse's behaviour. It could be criticised as loud and eccentric. Or it might be called highly individual, refreshing and strong-minded. But it could in no circumstances be called pro-German.

Cussen's views about the Wodehouses' behaviour, however changed between the time of writing his report in September 1944 and January 1945. On 15th January he wrote in a memorandum to a Miss J. J. Nunn, a senior civil servant at the British Home Office, about the evidence, favourable to Wodehouse, given to him on 10th

January 1945 by the Austrian national, Freddie Kraus, captured in Paris and, in January 1945, in a British detention camp. This evidence is set out later in this book. The memorandum to Miss Nunn read as follows: "Freddie Kraus, an Austrian who is presently detained at Camp 020, has made a statement regarding Wodehouse which you may care to have for your file. I have sent a copy to the Director (of Public Prosecutions).

"There is no reason to suppose that Kraus is being other than truthful in this matter, and I think you will agree that what he has told us confirms the impression we have already formed about Wodehouse."

Cussen, therefore, found no acceptable evidence whatsoever that the Wodehouses, either Ethel or Plum, had behaved improperly. On the contrary, the contemporary evidence was precisely to the contrary: the Wodehouses had behaved quietly and correctly.

Four important statements of evidence as to the behaviour of the Wodehouses were taken down in writing by Cussen and were included in the file which the Home Office made available to me in 1980. The first statement was from Marcel Vidal, the manager of the Hotel Bristol, Paris, where the Wodehouses had stayed since 11th September 1943. This statement dated 13th September 1944, read as follows:

"Mr. and Mrs. P. G. Wodehouse arrived in this hotel on September 11th 1943.

"They had not reserved rooms personally in advance as far as I can remember, but I think they were 'recommended' by some German authority.

"The charge for the two rooms they have occupied commenced at 500 francs. It varied with a change of rooms and it has been 240, 290, and finally as it is today 340 francs.

"They pay for their meals separately The charge for dinner at night would be for the two of them about 150 francs.

"They had their meals in the 'diplomatic dining room'. We had been asked by the German authorities to see that the Wodehouses were well looked after. I cannot say exactly which official made this request. Mrs. Wodehouse asked M. Jammet, the proprietor of the hotel, if she and her husband would be wise to use the diplomatic room. He said that he saw no harm in it. I know that he considered that they had better use that room as the food there was far better than in our ordinary restaurant. Moreover, if they went out to outside restaurants they would be charged exorbitant prices.

"While in the hotel they have led a very quiet life. We have not remarked that they have mixed with the Germans staying in the hotel.

"Mr. Werner Plack, a German official, frequently stayed in this hotel. I have seen him in conversation with the Wodehouses but so far as I could judge not in a very intimate way.

"I also remember that a German General once asked after them and said he hoped they were comfortable.

"But in general they did not have many friends visiting them. Apart from ordinary courtesies they did not speak to many people. Neither of them discussed the war or political subjects with the staff here and we have never heard of them doing so with guests. Mr. Wodehouse is a particularly quiet man.

"This statement has been read over to me and it is true. I would like to add that during the few weeks preceding the arrival of the Allied forces in Paris, Mr. and Mrs. Wodehouse showed no anxiety and there was no nervousness whatever on their part."

It is worth noting as a reinforcement and confirmation of the statement by the manager of the Hotel Bristol, Marcel Vidal, that the Wodehouses showed "no anxiety" and "no nervousness whatever" about the arrival of the Allied forces in Paris, that Wodehouse got in touch with the Allies within 24 hours of the liberation and also wrote to the British Home Secretary, Herbert Morrison, pleading for a chance to prove his innocence of the grave charges made against him. This letter, sent from the Hotel Bristol in Paris and dated 4th September 1944, read as follows:

"Sir – In view of the fact that on numerous occasions, through official and other channels, charges of great seriousness have been brought against me, I am hastening to report to you my presence here.

"This is not the occasion for me to make a detailed statement, but may I be allowed to say that the reports in the press that I obtained my release from internment by agreeing to broadcast on the German radio are entirely without foundation. The five talks which I delivered were arranged for after my release, and were made at my own suggestion.

"That it was criminally foolish of me to speak on the German radio, I admit. But my only motive in doing so was to give my American readers a humorous description of my adventures, as some response to the great number of letters which I had received from them while I was in camp. The five talks covered the five phases of my imprisonment, were purely comic in tone, and were designed to show to American listeners a group of Englishmen keeping up their spirits and courage under difficult conditions.

"You will understand that my present position is a highly embarrassing one, and I am most anxious to do everything possible to clear it up. I should be most grateful to you if you would let me know when I may have the opportunity of doing so.

"Meanwhile, unless you desire my presence in England, I will remain at the above address and keep in touch with the British authorities here.

I am, Sir,

Yours obediently (Sgd.) P. G. Wodehouse."

The second statement about Wodehouse's behaviour, undated, but almost certainly made in mid-September 1944, was from Aage Lonholt-Lipse, a Danish company director, living in Paris, and read as follows:

"In September 1943 I met the Wodehouses – by chance at the home of a friend of mine – I think it was at a Swedish gathering of some kind.

"I felt a sympathy for them and in addition my wife and I had had previous friendship with English people before the war.

"I have known the Wodehouses since that time and I have followed their life fairly closely.

"They have been living at the Hotel Bristol and – perhaps unwisely – they have not been mixing with the Americans also living there.

"I think I am right in saying that they lived a very solitary life at the 'Bristol'.

"From my knowledge of conditions in Paris hotels I should say that the Wodehouses did not receive any preferential treatment. They certainly had no extra supplies of butter or tea or meat or eggs.

"Very soon after our meeting the Wodehouses raised the question of money with me. I said I would do what I could; unhappily for various reasons it was not possible for me to assist them.

"I have given certain information to Major Cussen which is true and which I am prepared to repeat at any time."

The third statement, written in French, was from Gustav Elm, the Paris correspondent of the Swedish newspaper Svenska Dagbladet, and dated 14th September 1944. It should be noted that Elm describes as "sensational and false" the account given in the Swedish newspaper Aftonbladet – referred to earlier – that the Wodehouses had played "a prominent part in social life" during the war. Elm's evidence, confirming by letter what he had already given to Cussen verbally, read as follows:

"Dear Major Cussen – It is with pleasure that I repeat here what I told you yesterday by word of mouth on the subject of Mr. P. G. Wodehouse.

"I made the acquaintance of Mr. Wodehouse shortly after his arrival in Paris, and I have been very happy to see him and his wife on several occasions during the months which have passed. I ought to add that I have been for a long time a great admirer of his books.

"When I met Mr. Wodehouse for the first time he was somewhat reserved in his attitude towards me, and this was due, as he afterwards explained to me, to a very disagreeable recollection, arising from his stay in Berlin, which he had of a Swedish journalist who, having interviewed him, had published in his paper (I think it was Aftonbladet) a sensational but false article which did a great deal of harm to Mr. Wodehouse.

"From the beginning of our acquaintance Mr. Wodehouse and also his wife frequently questioned me as to my opinion on the end of the war and if I believed that an Allied landing would come to deliver them, allowing them to see their native country once again and their friends about whom they were anxious, being without news.

"I cannot recollect having on any occasion whatever heard sympathy for the German political regime expressed by Mr. Wodehouse and I have a strong impression that he has always remained a true Englishman.

"Mr. Wodehouse's books are very much appreciated by the Swedish public and indeed a translation of his last book became this spring one of the 'best sellers' in Sweden. I was very glad to be able to tell him this. Naturally, as the readers of Swedish papers were inter-

78

ested in him, on several occasions during the war their correspondents in London had sent news of references in the British press to Mr. Wodehouse. Thus it was that at the beginning of this summer the London correspondent of my paper, the Svenska Dagbladet, cabled that some friends of Mr Wodehouse had come to his defence and had expressed their conviction that he would never, knowingly, have acted against England as was the accusation against him. I remember that he was much affected by this news which allowed him to look forward to his rehabilitation.

"I have set out above the details which I remember. There are perhaps others which I may remember later and I will inform you of them if you wish it. To sum up, I would say that Mr. Wodehouse represented to me everything which is understood in England by the word 'gentleman' and all that this word means to English people.

Yours faithfully, (Sgd.) Gustav Elm.
Paris Correspondent of Svenska Dagbladet."

The fourth piece of evidence, dated 10th January 1945, was from the Austrian, Freddie Kraus, mentioned above. His statement, written in his own hand, read as follows:

"Concerning P. G. Wodehouse
"In December 1942 [*This must be an error by Kraus for 1943.*] I met Mr. and Mrs. P. G. Wodehouse at a dinner given by Dr. Kurt Josten at the house of Jussuf Saki Bey in Paris, 14 rue Pierre ler. du Serbie. My wife and I frequently asked Mr and Mrs Wodehouse to our home and introduced them to our friends and acquaintances. We were also frequently invited to the Wodehouses in the Hotel Bristol.

"I asked Mr. Wodehouse one day how he came to be a German prisoner. He told me that he and his wife had arranged with the English Consul in Le Touquet in May 1940, that the latter could let Wodehouse know in good time should the Germans advance further, in order that Wodehouse would be able to get away in good time to England. He was just listening to the B.B.C. news stating that the Germans had been thrown back when the first German soldiers appeared. He was thereupon taken prisoner and put into an internment camp.

"Mrs. Wodehouse told me one day that her husband had broadcast on the German radio and this had made a very bad impression in England; he had only intended to give English listeners a description of life in an internment camp and had never thought that this might be taken as pro-German propaganda. The moment she heard of these broadcasts, she had begged him to stop giving them at once, but only after he had already spoken a few times. As soon as he realised the significance of his action, he had written a statement and sent it to the Home Office.

"In February or March 1943, Mr. Wodehouse asked me whether I would accompany him to the Gestapo (S.D.), rue Saussaye, to act as his interpreter. He had received a summons to appear there, had already called there three times, and been sent away. He could not understand the people, and they could not understand him. At the S.D. we had to go to the registration department dealing with foreigners under observation (I do not remember the number). I learned there that Mr. and Mrs. Wodehouse were supposed to report every week, entering their names in a book. Hitherto, Wodehouse had always been sent away as his file had not yet reached that department. I had identified myself with my German pass, and said to the clerk that I had met Wodehouse only a short time before, and would like to know what there was against him and how his case stood, also whether I could be seen about with him. He told me that he had seen from the file that 'Wodehouse was the English Goethe about whom several big-wigs in the Foreign Office in Berlin had made fools of themselves; Wodehouse was considered quite harmless and orders had been received to leave him in peace.' The clerk then gave permission for Mr. Wodehouse to report only once a month, and that he could also sign for his wife.

"Through Mr. Wodehouse, at a dinner, I met Mr. Werner Plack, member of the Press Department of the German Embassy in Paris. I chatted with him about Wodehouse. Plack told me that the intention had been to use Wodehouse for propaganda purposes, but he had refused, after having spoken a few times, to broadcast any more on the German radio. As he was a perfectly harmless humourist who had gained international fame through his work, Wodehouse had not again been interned."

*　　*　　*

By the time Kraus made this statement in Wodehouse's favour, on 10th January 1945, the Director of Public Prosecutions in London had already decided that no evidence had been found to justify prosecution of Wodehouse. On 23rd November 1944, Theobald Mathew (later Sir Theobald) the Director of Public Prosecutions, sent an important memorandum to the Home Office, the full text of which read as follows:

"Having considered Major Cussen's report, I have informed M.I.5 that I am satisfied, on the present material, that there is not sufficient evidence to justify a prosecution of this man.

"It is possible that information may subsequently come to light, which will establish a more sinister motive for this man's activities in Germany but, having regard to the nature and content of his broadcasts, there is, at the moment, nothing to justify any action on my part; nor do I consider that the Trading with the Enemy Regulations would apply to this man's business transactions with the enemy while he was in enemy, or enemy-occupied, territory."

It was this opinion upon which Sir Donald Somervell, the British Attorney-General, based his speech in the House of Commons of 15th December 1944, rejecting a demand for the prosecution of Wodehouse by Quintin Hogg, M.P.

Nonetheless, although the Attorney-General in this speech said there was not sufficient evidence to prosecute Wodehouse in the courts on the charge of treason, or on the lesser charge of trading with the enemy, he did so in such a legalistic manner that anyone listening to the debate, or reading it afterwards, would certainly not have been convinced of Wodehouse's innocence. The impression given by Somervell was merely that sufficient evidence of guilt could not be found. In a court of law, this is indeed sufficient for a verdict of innocence to be returned; but in the court of public opinion this is not so, and certainly was not so in Wodehouse's case. Somervell's speech did not convince the general public that Wodehouse was innocent, nor was it meant to do so.

At the time, Somervell could not be blamed for speaking as he did in the House of Commons. Nonetheless, given that after Somervell spoke, Cussen officially continued his search for evidence on the Wodehouse affair, and given that such later evidence, like that of Kraus, confirmed Wodehouse's own account of events – as Cussen himself said in his memorandum to Miss Nunn of the Home Office of

15th January 1945 – such evidence of Wodehouse's innocence should, in all fairness, have been made public in an appropriate manner.

It was a tragedy for Wodehouse that Cussen himself appears to have become so convinced of Wodehouse's innocence that he did not consider it necessary to collate in written form, and in one file, all the evidence of innocence which came to light through his investigations after his original report of 28th September 1944. That Cussen did receive such further evidence is certain: for example, Jacqueline Grant, as she herself told me, was interviewed by Cussen in 1945 and corroborated Wodehouse's claims of innocence. Yet no such evidence appeared in the Home Office file when I read it in 1980. Nor did Cussen, or those instructing him, consider it necessary to pursue enquiries later in Germany, to establish the truth, although the American authorities, for example, did seek out Werner Plack in 1948 to give evidence in a case involving an American citizen.

It may be said that Cussen, and the Director of Public Prosecutions, and the Home Office, were concerned with only one thing: whether sufficient evidence existed against Wodehouse that might lead to a successful prosecution; and that no such evidence being discovered, their task was at an end. This was, in fact, the view that was taken. Nonetheless, although that may have accorded with the legal obligation, there surely existed a *moral* obligation on the British Government – since it was a Government Department that had instigated the denouncement of Wodehouse on the B.B.C. in 1941 – to make public all such evidence of Wodehouse's innocence as Cussen had uncovered.

*   *   *

Why did Wodehouse himself never make greater efforts to clear his own name in public? He was certainly advised to do so latterly – though not at first – by Cussen, who came to believe more and more strongly in Wodehouse's innocence as time went by. Wodehouse could certainly have had published his own account of what happened to him between 1940 and 1945, had he insisted with his publishers. Or else he could have sued for libel any of those newspapers which had, during the war and after, printed stories bringing him into hatred, ridicule or contempt – not in order to get damages from them but to get the truth on the record. Yet Wodehouse did neither of these things.

He did, however, take, or allow to be taken on his behalf, the following public actions. First, he gave several press interviews, of which, unfortunately, the only reasonably comprehensive one was with the journalist Hubert Cole in the Illustrated magazine on 7th December 1946, from which other extracts have already been quoted. In this there occurs the following passages:

"Cole: It has been suggested that, for some sinister reason you were given preferential treatment in the German concentration camps, and that you were released because you promised to broadcast for the Germans.

"Wodehouse: I had exactly the same treatment as all other prisoners in the camp. I lived in a room with 66 other men – the salt of the earth, if I may say so – and had the same food, if you call it food. The question of broadcasting was never mentioned while I was in camp. I was released, like all the men in our crowd who had reached that age, because I was 60 years old.

"Cole: Is it true that the German Government paid all your expenses at the Adlon Hotel?

"Wodehouse: Not so much as a mark or a pfennig. Some Jewish friends of ours lent us a considerable sum to be repaid in England after the war, and my wife sold her jewellery.

"Cole: Why did you make the broadcasts?

"Wodehouse: I was not allowed to write to anyone except my wife, and I wanted to express my gratitude to the scores of American readers of my books who had written me letters and sent me parcels. The broadcasts consisted entirely of five humorous descriptions of my experiences as an internee. I knew that many British prisoners-of-war had broadcast from Germany to reassure their families of their safety, so I assumed that there could be nothing wrong in my doing this . . .

"Cole: Did you have any idea that your broadcasts would be regarded as pro-Nazi propaganda?

"Wodehouse: No. Considering that they were all about how we were packed in cattle trucks by the Nazis and taken for journeys lasting for three days and three nights, with nothing but a small bowl of soup per day, and how we used to eat matches because there was nothing else to eat, I did not.

"Cole: What do you think of those talks now?

"Wodehouse: I realise that they were a ghastly blunder and that I was a complete fool to have made them. But I simply had no idea at the time that they could be mistaken for anything other than what I intended them to be – a gesture of gratitude to my unknown friends in America. There was not a word in the five talks which could not have been printed in any English paper.

"Cole: Did you try to put the matter straight?

"Wodehouse: Immediate steps. I got the Swiss Embassy to forward a statement to the British Government, explaining how the blunder had occurred and reaffirming my loyalty. I also applied for permission to leave Germany and to return to England via Palestine on a train which was going there, in order to make my answer in person. But this was not granted.

"Cole: What steps did you take to regularise your position at the end of the war?

"Wodehouse: In 1943 the Germans allowed me to go to live under supervision in Paris. The day after the Liberation I reported to the American colonel in charge of a party of advance troops and asked him to inform the British authorities of my whereabouts, so that an inquiry could be made. An official from the Home Office came over from London and took down a full statement from me, going into my case in minute detail in a series of interviews which lasted two weeks. After reading this statement, Sir Donald Somervell, the then Attorney-General, stated in the House of Commons in December 1944 that I was clear of all charges of collaboration. In reply to a question in the House, Mr. Anthony Eden said: 'There is no question of a charge. The matter has been gone into, and there are no grounds upon which we could take action.' I have also received a formal clearance from the French authorities.

"Cole: What do you think of the reaction in Britain – the banning of your books in public libraries and so on?

"Wodehouse: I can understand the feeling against me being bitter in 1941, but I hope that, having now learned the true and full facts, people will understand that my action was never intended to be disloyal, though nobody appreciates more deeply than I how foolish it was . . ."

Secondly, Wodehouse instigated a letter from R. T. Rees, in his old school magazine The Alleynian, published in July 1945. This letter read as follows:

"Sir – I have received from Mr. P. G. Wodehouse a letter which is too long for publication in full. But extracts from it might interest your readers. It begins:

" 'I had a letter from Bill Townend a few days ago, handing me on the gist of a letter which you wrote to him regarding the feeling at Dulwich about me. He writes: "Rees says he feels you ought to know that Dulwich opinion regarding the broadcasts is very critical, even hostile, because the general idea is that you were persuaded to broadcast by the Nazis in order to add interest to their propaganda in return for some measure of liberty, and that what is needed is a brief account of what actually happened."

" 'I don't know if you have read a book by Harry Flannery called – I think – "Berlin Assignment", in which he states that a representative of the German propaganda office came to see me in camp and arranged with me that I should be released in order to broadcast. This is absolutely untrue. I never received such a visit, nor was I ever approached on the matter. It was not until after my release that the subject of broadcasting came up.

" 'What happened was this. I was released on June 21, 1941, a few months before I was 60. I should have been released automatically on reaching the age of 60, and I imagine that I was given my freedom a little earlier because of the agitation which had been going on in America for my release.'

"Mr. Wodehouse gives instances of this agitation, and proceeds:

" 'On arrival in Berlin I ran into a very old friend of mine, a German who had been at Hollywood with me. I was telling him about life in camp, and a friend of his, who joined us, suggested that I might like to broadcast an account of my experiences to my American readers. It was so exactly what I wanted to do that I jumped at the idea. All through the last ten months of my internment I had been receiving letters from American readers, very anxious to know how I was getting on and I had not been able to answer any of these, as in camp you are allowed to write only to near relatives. I felt that these people, not knowing the circumstances, would be thinking me ungrateful and ungracious for ignoring their letters, and it seemd to me that by broadcasting my experiences I could make a sort of interim acknowledgement. I can honestly say that it never occurred to me for a moment that there was anything wrong in using the German radio as a medium for getting in touch with people in America to whom I was very grateful. (Some of them had sent me parcels.) I can see now, of course, how idiotic it was of me to do such a thing and I naturally regret it very much, but at the time it never struck me that I was doing anything wrong.

" 'While in camp I had roughed out a humorous book about camp life, and I condensed this material into five talks, covering the five phases of my internment – the first week in Loos prison, the second week in Liége barracks, the next five weeks at Huy citadel and the rest of the time at Tost in Upper Silesia, starting with a description of my arrest at Le Touquet. I recorded these talks on wax and went off to stay in the country and thought no more about it. It was only when my wife arrived in Berlin on July 28, just after the last talk had been broadcast, that I heard of the reaction in England.

" 'I see now, of course, that I was tricked into making these talks, and I naturally feel a damned fool, but I hope I have made it clear that there was never anything in the nature of a bargain with the Germans. I was released before there was any suggestion of a broadcast, and there was never any idea that my freedom was dependent on my broadcasting.

" 'This, fortunately, I can prove. Just after my last talk I received a cable from the editor of the Saturday Evening Post, who was considering for serial publication my novel "Money in the Bank", which I had written in camp. He said he liked the story and was anxious to buy it, but could do so only on my giving him my assurance that I would stop talking on the German radio. I replied that I had already stopped, that I had never intended to do more than these five humorous descriptions of camp life and that he could be perfectly easy in his mind, as I would not speak again on any subject whatsoever. A week or so later I heard from him that he had bought the story, and it started running as a serial in November.

" 'Now this cable of mine, of which I have given you the gist, was handed to an official of the Wilhelmstrasse and sent off by him, and if there had ever been any idea that I had been released because of an agreement on my part to broadcast German propaganda, I hardly think the German authorities would have made no protest when I announced that I was through after giving five talks mostly about how I read Shakespeare while in camp and how internees who had no tobacco smoked tea. If I had made such an agreement they would undoubtedly have tried to hold me to it and sent me back to camp if I refused to carry it out. But they did nothing, and I went on living unmolested in the country. Eventually I was allowed to come to Paris.

" 'I gather there has been a great deal of indignation in England because I was supposed to be living at the Adlon Hotel, presumably at the expense of the German Government. I stayed at the Adlon for a month or two each winter because they would not let me stay anywhere else, and when there I paid all my own expenses. My wife got more than enough to pay our way through the sale of her jewellery. From early April till December each year we had no expenses as we were living in the country at the home of a relation of the Hollywood friend I mentioned earlier. When we came to Paris, I was able to get 350,000 francs from my Spanish publisher, and also to borrow from friends. I would never have been in Berlin at all, if it had been possible to go on living in the country. But the house there had to be closed during the winter on account of heating difficulties.

" 'While in Berlin I hardly spoke to a German. I was very busy writing – I wrote three novels and ten short stories while in Germany – and our friends were a few English and American women married to or the widows of Germans.'

"Mr. Wodehouse says that he has already given this account to Government officials, but he would like to have the main facts published in The Alleynian.

I am, Sir, Yours, etc. R. T. Rees."

Thirdly, Wodehouse wrote a letter to the show business newspaper, Variety, which appeared on 8th May 1946. Parts of this letter read as follows:

"Editor, Variety – I can't tell you what pleasure it was to get your letter this afternoon and how grateful I am for your offer to give me some of your space for my story. I have been one of Variety's most assiduous and enthusiastic readers for more than 30 years, and there is no paper in the world in which I would rather put my case. Yours is just the public whose opinion I most value.

"When I came out of camp I wrote a book about my experiences as an internee, the second chapter of which dealt with the broadcasts. I had hoped to publish this as my first postwar production, but

Doubleday, my publishers, advised putting it off for a while and are bringing out a 'Jeeves' novel in the early fall.

"I think the trouble all along has been that nobody in the United States heard the broadcasts and this uproar in England gave to the American public the impression that they were in some way pro-German, if not actual German propaganda. In fact, they were merely a humorous description of camp life, designed purely to amuse my American readers and could have been printed as they stood in any American or English paper.

"In support of this statement I should like to quote a letter I received this morning from a man in England, a stranger to me, who said that he had been a prisoner-of-war for two and a half years and that it was reading my books that kept up the spirits of the men in his camp. He says:

" 'I would like to tell you that having read your broadcasts I cannot see how anyone could possibly see anything in the slightest pro-German or anti-British in them. But I will not give you my own opinion, I will tell you that of the late Air Marshal Boyd. I was his personal assistant and we were prisoners together in Italy. He read your broadcasts and gave them to me saying: "Why the Germans ever let him say all this I cannot think. They have either got more sense of humour than I credited them with or it has just slipped past the censor. There is some stuff about being packed in cattle trucks and a thing about Loos jail that you would think would send a Hun crazy. Wodehouse has probably been shot by now." '

"I think the opinion of a British Air Marshal who knew what was in the talks ought to carry more weight than that of British newspapermen who didn't. But unfortunately it was the views of the latter that reached the public ..."

Fourthly, Wodehouse allowed his old school friend Bill Townend to publish the letters which he, Wodehouse, had written to him over a period of 33 years from 1920–1953, and in some of the later letters Wodehouse does deal in passing with certain of the accusations against him. But he is writing letters to a friend, not systematically working his way through the years 1940 to 1945 by chronology or by accusation. Wodehouse never expected his letters to be published and when he touches on the subject of his internment, release and broadcasts, he writes, for the most part, lightheartedly – though certainly at times with strong, if understated, feeling. For example the broadcast with Flannery, and Flannery's subsequent book, "Assignment to Berlin", which was seriously unpleasant about Wodehouse, is briefly and casually mentioned, and the book dismissed as "bilge", but without much trouble taken to prove that it was "bilge".

Few of the references in the letters to Townend about allegations made by other people concerning Wodehouse's war-time activities are very long, and usually appear sandwiched between lengthier passages on other matters. There is no methodical analysis of the charges made against him, and no methodical destruction of them. For the most part, he clearly assumes that Townend would know that he was incapable of anything dishonourable or treasonable, and leaves it at that. However, in a letter of 18th April 1953, the letter, incidentally, in which he gave Townend permission to publish his previous letters to him, as well as some extracts from the camp diaries which he had kept, Wodehouse wrote at some length, to rebut the charges against him: "You ask, Do I approve of your publishing this book with all the stuff about my German troubles? Certainly. But mark this, laddie, I don't suppose that anything you say or anything I say will make the slightest damn bit of difference. You need dynamite to dislodge an idea that has got itself firmly rooted in the public mind.

"When I was interned, a man on Time, sitting down to write something picturesque and amusing about me, produced the following:

'When the German army was sweeping toward Paris last Spring "Plum" (to his friends) was throwing a cocktail-party in the jolly old pine woods at Le Touqet. Suddenly a motor-cycle Gendarme tore up, shouted, "the Germans will be here in an hour", tore off. The guests, thoroughly familiar with this sort of drollery from Wodehouse novels, continued to toss down cocktails. The Germans arrived punctually, first having taken care to block all the roads. They arrested the Wodehouses and guests, later permitted Mrs. Wodehouse and celebrants to depart southward.'

You wouldn't think anyone would have believed such an idiotic story, but apparently everyone did. In 1941 someone wrote in the Daily Express:

'He lived in Le Touquet. He was drinking a cocktail when the Germans arrived, and he was led away quite happily into captivity.'

And in 1945 someone else thus in the Daily Mail:

'He was, in fact, just sinking a cocktail when, in 1940, someone dashed in and cried that the Germans would be there in an hour or less. The party stayed put with a phlegm worthy of Drake's game of bowls.'

So after four years the thing was still going as strong as ever, and presumably still is. It is embedded in the world's folklore, and nothing will ever get it out. I wonder where I am supposed to have collected these light-hearted guests whom I am described as entertaining. By the time the Germans were threatening Paris, the resident population of Le Touquet had shrunk so considerably that the most determined host would have found it impossible to assemble even the nucleus of a cocktail-party, and the few of us who had been unable to get away were not at all in the mood for revelry. We were pensive and preoccupied, starting at sudden noises and trying to overcome the illusion of having swallowed a heaping teaspoonful of butterflies.

"Odd, too, that a motor-cycle Gendarme should have torn up and shouted, 'The Germans will be here in an hour' when they had been there two months. They entered Le Touquet on May 22nd. I was interned on July 21st. At the time when the incident is supposed to have taken place we were all confined to our houses except when we went to Paris Plage to report at the Kommandatur to a German Kommandant who had a glass eye . . ."

Wodehouse then went on in passages quoted earlier, to complain how journalists had embroidered what he said to the point where his whole meaning had been distorted; or else had invented stories, such as that he was giving a cocktail-party when the Germans arrived.

The fifth occasion when Wodehouse wrote publicly in his own defence was in a letter to Encounter magazine in October 1954, when that magazine printed what purported – wrongly – to be the text of the Berlin broadcasts. The version published by Encounter is substantially different from the original texts given in this book, which are taken from contemporary German transcripts.

Wodehouse's rebuttal in Encounter of the charges against him was certainly unambiguous, but it was also amusing rather than systematic. The relevant part of the passage is as follows:

"The idea of finally seeing my five Berlin broadcasts in print appeals to me. You would have thought that by this time, taking into consideration the fact that I am on excellent terms with the British, French, and American Governments, and that the B.B.C. and I are like Heloise and Abelard, people would have realised that there could not have been anything very subversive in them. But not so. There was a review of a recent book of mine in one of the papers over here (i.e., the U.S.A.) which began:

'Pelham Grenville Wodehouse, whom Sinclair Lewis once described as "master of the touchingly inane", is in midseason form this time. These ten short stories, gathered together under the title of "Nothing Serious", are just what the doctor ordered for that great multitude of admirers on both sides of the Atlantic who for more than a generation have got the sheerest delight from a Wodehouseian humour that is something apart from any other fun-writing in the literature. (Yes, I know. Fine so far. Couldn't be better. Puts in a nutshell just what I was thinking myself. But get the next paragraph.)

'Gone are the memories of the nightmare which was visited upon him in World War II, when his Nazi captors persuaded him to broadcast from his Upper Silesian prison appeals to his British countrymen to surrender to the Madman of Berchtesgaden.'

Twelve years ago, when I was a slip of a boy of 60, a crack like that would have cut me to the quick, but one advantage of being a septuagenarian is that you don't cut easy. When there is so little time left and one may cease ticking over at any moment, it seems silly to worry about anything. Nowadays I'm like the fellow who said he didn't much mind what people wrote about him in the papers, so long as they spelled the name right.

"Still, if that is the story that is going the round of the clubs, it might be as well to print the broadcasts just for the record."

Yet, convincing in tone and argument though such passages are, so far as they go, neither they, nor anything else that Wodehouse made public in his lifetime, amounted to a methodical and thorough rebuttal of the charges of Nazi sympathies, cowardice and treason.

The reasons why he took no adequate action either immediately or later to clear his name seem to be several.

First, in September 1944, Cussen specifically and unambiguously instructed Wodehouse not to give interviews to the press. Later, when Cussen himself had reversed his opinion and had come to believe in Wodehouse's innocence, he advised him to take action to clear his own name, but by that time certain close British friends advised him otherwise. They also advised him, in the immediate aftermath of the war, not even to return to Britain for the time being. The argument of Wodehouse's friends against him returning was that feeling in the United Kingdom against him, however wrongly based, was very strong, and they believed that if he were to be closely exposed to it, it would cause him more pain. The Home Office, as once secret documents in their dossier on Wodehouse show, did not wish him to return to the United Kingdom after Paris was liberated, as they were not certain about some legal technicalities regarding Wodehouse's property and funds. Thus there was both official and unofficial pressure on Wodehouse not to return to London.

Secondly, his American and British publishers specifically advised him that for commercial reasons – namely, that sales of his books might be adversely affected – it would be better to do nothing further, and let the affair blow over. Wodehouse had written an account of his experiences in the four internment camps – provisionally entitled "Wodehouse in Wonderland" – but both Doubledays, his American publisher, and Herbert Jenkins, his British publisher, advised him not to publish anything which would stir matters up. They persuaded him that the first book that should appear under his name after the war should be a Jeeves novel.

However, some of those who believed in Wodehouse's innocence definitely did not agree that the best course was to do nothing about clearing his name publicly. One such person was Scott Meredith, an American writer who became Wodehouse's agent in 1946. While serving in the U.S. Air Force, Meredith had written to Wodehouse – although he did not know him other than through his work – and had received a courteous reply, giving Wodehouse's version of the Berlin broadcasts. Meredith then wrote the following letter in the autumn of 1945 to Wodehouse's American lawyer, Watson Washburn:

"I am aware that there is a school of thought which states that the

92

best way to restore Wodehouse to his former position is to say absolutely nothing about him at all in the public press until the whole thing dies down of its own accord. I hope you are not of this school, I certainly am not.

"The thing will never die down of its own accord – not enough to matter, at any rate. There are far too many people who read hurriedly about the Wodehouse broadcasts – hurriedly because they were anxious to turn to the stories of men who had cut their wives into six neat pieces, and of Explosions Which Kill Ten – and now think of Wodehouse only as a Nazi collaborationist. If you delve into it you learn that they remember so little of what they read that they can't quite tell you why they think so: but they remember that they think of Wodehouse as a collaborationist because he broadcast for the Germans – but who do not know that the broadcasts were light, non-political talks about his experiences. It is amazing how many of them are positive that they read somewhere that the Wodehouse talks were certainly political, and that, in fact, he advised the British and Americans to give up. (Ridiculous, of course, when you know that he did not broadcast to the British, and the Americans were not then at war with the Germans: but so very, very many people have told it to me that way.) Then there are the people who are somewhat better informed, and who know that the broadcasts were non-political, but who believe he is guilty because he was warned after each broadcast of the furor he was causing in England and America, and still continued with the series.

"These people must be told the facts of the case – the actual facts. They must be told that the broadcasts were non-political; that he was not warned between broadcasts because the airings were recorded and he therefore did not stay around Berlin, making them in person and talking to American correspondents all the time; and that he has been labelled by the British government itself as merely 'injudicious, but obviously not a German collaborationist'."

Sadly, this excellent advice was not followed. Wodehouse allowed himself to be persuaded by others, who, in his view, had their finger more closely on the pulse of British and American public opinion: it seems that he reasoned to himself that, after all, he had badly misjudged British and American public opinion before, at the time of the original Berlin broadcasts, and he would be well advised now to accept the advice of other people who appeared in better touch with the current situation than he who had spent five years away from the United Kingdom and United States; other people who genuinely believed they were acting in his best interests, both in personal and commercial terms.

There was a third reason why Wodehouse did not comprehensively and publicly rebut the accusations. Although he was undoubtedly restive at the policy of silence advocated by his publishers, by most of his friends, and by the British authorities – hence his actions with Variety and Illustrated – Wodehouse was not wholly unwilling to be persuaded not to rake over the whole affair in detail. He had a strong temperamental aversion against involving himself in anything disagreeable and distasteful, such as raking over in public the events of the last five years was likely to be. By the end of the war, he was only weeks short of his 64th birthday, and had been, for over four years, under a unique variety of exceptional physical and mental strains: after all, he had been bombed, arrested, interned, lost 42 lbs in weight while in internment, been widely and loudly accused of being a traitor to his country, been forced to live with no regular source of income in an enemy country, been arrested again, been interrogated by his own country's security services on grave suspicion of treason, an offence which carried the death penalty, and learnt of the death of his beloved daughter, Leonora.

Some of those who knew him said that he did not do anything adequate to clear his name because he was not in fact deeply affected by the affair. According to the evidence I have collected, this is wrong. I believe that Wodehouse was indeed deeply hurt, exactly as he wrote in his evidence to Cussen: "I have suffered a great deal of mental pain as a result of my action." Naturally, he did his best to conceal his hurt under silence, or under the occasional light-hearted reference, because concealing emotions in general, and pain in particular, was part of the personal and social code in which he was brought up and which he admired – the traditional British code of the stiff upper lip. Malcolm Muggeridge, who was the first British officer from the security services to see him in Paris in 1944, before Cussen began his official investigation, was right when he wrote in his essay on Wodehouse in "Tread Softly For You Tread On My Jokes": "As with all imaginative people there is an area of inner reserve in Wodehouse which one never penetrates. The scars of his time in the stocks are hidden there." Those who said that Wodehouse did nothing much because he did not care much, failed to realise that there was such a reserve there to be penetrated.

It was significant, too, that Wodehouse never returned to the United Kingdom in the last 30 years of his life, although his wife did, and although he often said that he was planning to do so. Again, I believe Muggeridge was right about the reason for Wodehouse never returning to the country of his birth, when he wrote that Wodehouse's attitude was "like that of a man who has parted, in painful circumstances, from someone he loves, and whom he both longs and dreads to see again". Further evidence of how deeply Wodehouse felt was given to me by one of Wodehouse's last British editors, Christopher Maclehose, who wrote in a letter to me: "He hated the fact that when he was 90, reporters from the B.B.C. still seemed to be more interested in that part of his life (i.e. the war years) than in any other. The only time I saw him angry was when Ethel, in the wake of one of these B.B.C. intrusions, sought to correct the impression that they had lived cosily at the Adlon. Plum banged his palm on the table and said he didn't want any more said about it, he was sick of it, and that was that."

On this question of his attitude to his own country, Wodehouse made some interesting comments to a journalist, Peter Hastings, in New York in 1950. He said: " 'My England's gone. Blandings Castle, Bertie, Pongo, Lord Em. – they're all gone. Some people think they never existed. I don't know. I was frightfully fond of them anyway . . .' Hastings then asked him if it were true he was going to give up his British citizenship now that he was living in America. Wodehouse replied: 'Can't say at all . . . Not at all sure. What do you think?' It was an extraordinary question to put to an interviewing journalist (wrote Hastings) . . . I replied that it was none of my business but if he really wanted my opinion I thought it would possibly alienate millions of British Commonwealth readers . . . Wodehouse said: '. . . I must say I rather think you're right about becoming an American. One would feel somehow that one had let one's country down. And I'm still an Englishman – would be if I lived another 100 years in New York . . . Tell them (the journalist's readers) I'm going to remain a

British citizen. I feel all British people ought to stick together, now I give it a thought.' "

* * *

An understanding of Wodehouse's character is clearly crucial to any understanding of how he came to act as he did after his release from Tost.

There are those who say that Wodehouse was "naïve". But this does him an injustice. His character – as those who knew him well have described it to me – was more subtle, more complex and more elusive. For example, Thelma Cazalet-Keir (whose brother, Peter, married Wodehouse's daughter, Leonora) said to me: "He was not so much naïve as quite exceptionally good-natured and innocent." Evelyn Waugh, in his broadcast on the B.B.C. on 25th July 1961, to mark Wodehouse's 80th birthday, spoke of his "humility" and "beauty of character".

Wodehouse was most certainly not naïve in that he understood with exactness the commercial world in which he operated, notwithstanding certain comments by his daughter Leonora, quoted below. He not only understood it: he was remarkably, indeed uniquely, successful in operating in it himself. He was comprehensively practical, as his letters to Bill Townend in "Performing Flea" show, both in the craft of writing and in the commercial marketing of what he had written. He studied the needs of magazine and book publishers, and gave them what they wanted, and knew what he ought to be paid for what he gave them. Consider this passage from a letter to Townend regarding the sale of Wodehouse's short story, "The Crime Wave at Blandings", to George Lorimer, the editor of the Saturday Evening Post, in 1936: ". . . He (Lorimer) paid me $2,000 and wrote me a letter asking if that was all right. I wrote back, 'Dear Mr. Lorimer, I am so intensely spiritual that money means nothing to me, but I must confirm that $2,000 was a bit of a sock on the jaw, as I had always thought that a short story was supposed to fetch a tenth of the price of a serial, so I had been looking forward to $4,000.' This apparently touched his heart for the first thing he said to me when I came into the room was that he would give me $4,000."

To refute the simplistic description that Wodehouse was "naïve", however, it is not necessary to rely solely on evidence of the undoubted practical grasp he possessed of the publishing market. In his letters to Townend he reveals a shrewd and level-headed approach to other aspects of living. His comments on individuals, or situations, while usually amiable, are perceptive: the reader feels that Wodehouse's judgments are balanced and fair; that he has "got it right". Here is an extract, exemplifying this ability to judge shrewdly but fairly, from one of his letters to Townend, written from Paris in August 1945, in which Wodehouse is commenting on Townend's comparative lack of success as an author:

"I'll tell you what's the whole trouble with you, Bill, and that is that you have never done anything except write the stuff and are competing with all these birds who hang around authors' lunches and go about lecturing and presenting prizes at girls' schools. I don't think it matters in the long run, but there's no doubt that all these other fellows who shove themselves forward and suck up to the critics do get a lot of publicity, and it helps them for a while. I always think Hugh Walpole's reputation was two-thirds publicity. He was always endorsing books and speaking at lunches and so on.

"I can't remember if I ever told you about meeting Hugh when I was at Oxford getting my D.Litt. I was staying with the Vice-Chancellor at Magdalen and he blew in and spent the day. It was just after Hilaire Belloc had said that I was the best living English writer. It was just a gag, of course, but it worried Hugh terribly. He said to me, 'Did you see what Belloc said about you?' I said I had. 'I wonder why he said that.' 'I wonder,' I said. Long silence. 'I can't imagine why he said that,' said Hugh. I said I couldn't, either. Another long silence. 'It seems such an extraordinary thing to say!' 'Most extraordinary.' Long silence again. 'Ah, well,' said Hugh, having apparently found the solution, 'the old man's getting very old.'

"We went for a long walk in the afternoon, and he told me that when somebody wrote a stinker about some book of his, he cried for hours. Can you imagine getting all worked up about a bad notice? I always feel about the critics that there are bound to be quite a number of them who don't like one's stuff and one just has to accept it. They don't get a sob out of me.

"I never cared much for Walpole. There was a time when I

seemed about to be registered as number fourteen or something on his list of friends – did you know that he used to list all his friends in order? – but nothing came of it. He wanted me to come to Majorca with him, but I backed out and this probably shoved me down to number thirty or off the list altogether."

Wodehouse retained all his life much of the common sense attitudes and values of the normal, happy, and successful schoolboy he had been at Dulwich between 1894 and 1900. Writing to Bill Townend in 1953, Wodehouse described himself thus: "Mentally I seem not to have progressed a step since I was eighteen. With world convulsions happening every hour on the hour, I appear to be still the rather awkward lad I was, when we brewed our first cup of tea in our study together, my only concern the outcome of a rugby football match." There is much truth in that. Wodehouse did indeed possess the shrewd and robust common sense of a schoolboy, but the sophisticated cunning and sustained evil to be found in the adult world was something he did not, and did not wish, to comprehend.

Outside his own circle of friends, Wodehouse was a rather shy, quiet, and diffident man. Two examples well illustrate his shyness and diffidence. The first was given to me by Jacqueline Grant. She said that when he was living at Le Touquet before the Second World War, he used to go for a walk by himself, each day, in the nearby forest. On these walks, he was so shy that if he ever saw anyone approaching him down a forest path – and since he was so short-sighted he did not usually see them until they were very close – he would dodge behind a tree and hide, rather than engage in even the briefest greeting or conversation.

On these solitary walks, incidentally, Wodehouse would frequently break out into loud laughter as some comic thought struck him about the current story on which he was working.

Ethel Wodehouse was very different in character. She was not shy. As her secretary in 1940, Jacqueline Grant would accompany her on shopping expeditions to Paris Plage. Often, if Ethel Wodehouse saw some British officers there – usually from the Royal Air Force base nearby – she would walk up to them, introduce herself, and invite them to come for dinner or a party at Low Wood. Ethel Wodehouse would offer hospitality in this way, partly because she did indeed enjoy such social occasions, but partly and importantly, also, because she and her husband considered such hospitality as a contribution towards helping the morale of the British armed forces in France. During most of these occasions – apart from the actual dinner itself – Wodehouse would be working alone at his typewriter. But at some time during the evening, while the others were dancing to the gramophone, he would show his face around the door and ask, as Jacqueline Grant described it to me, "with that friendly, short-sighted look, and sweet smile": "Is everybody happy?" The guests would always call out "Yes", and invite him to join them. He would always shake his head, smiling, and say he must get on with his work.

The second example of his diffidence comes from Wodehouse himself.

When Wodehouse was a journalist on The Globe, in London, between 1902 and 1909, he was once despatched to interview Winston Churchill. Recalling it afterwards, he confessed: "I got into a frightful dither about it. Called at the door. Asked for Mr. Winston Churchill, please. Most fortunate thing in the world, you know – the butler said he was in his bath. Would never have known what to say to him!"

The views of two other people about Wodehouse's character are interesting and relevant in light of the subsequent, war-time events. In the issue of Strand magazine of February 1927, the journalist Augustus Muir described Wodehouse thus: "A big, broad, ruddy, clear-eyed fellow; an open-air man, no hater of wind and rain; in his day, a boxer, swimmer, cricketer, rugby player; a kindly, easy, matey, shy sort of chap, like a senior public-school boy who refuses to grow older . . . Quite unsophisticated . . . Good nature: that is the key-note of the man and his work . . . One of the most unspoilt fellows I have ever met."

Wodehouse's daughter, Leonora, whom he greatly loved, and who greatly loved him, wrote this affectionate but shrewd description of him in 1929: "Nothing is a pleasure to him that involves pain to anything . . . (He has) an overpowering hatred of hurting people . . . He has a quality of sweetness . . . Kindliness is your first and last impression of him." She also added: "He has simply no idea of business or anything connected with it . . . Mummie looks after all his interests and is very clever about it."

These views of Wodehouse's character help to explain why he acted as he did, when the Germans asked him if he would like to broadcast in 1941: it is clear that Wodehouse was himself so genuinely decent a person that, until it was demonstrated to him to the contrary, he tended to react as though other people were similarly decent. He did not readily see evil in others. He did not expect duplicity or cunning. Being himself friendly he expected friendliness in others.

Let me give two examples which illustrate, in different spheres, his unusually trusting nature. The first example describes a visit to Wodehouse's temporary flat in London, by his friend and collaborator in various stage productions, Guy Bolton, quoted in "Bring on the Girls" by Bolton and Wodehouse: "His (Wodehouse's) flat was on the fourth floor. There was no lift and Guy, travel-tired, toiled up the long staircase to arrive somewhat breathless as he entered the already opened door. Plum had just finished a letter and he called out a cheery 'Hurray, you're here. Just a tick while I get this letter off.' So saying he walked to the half-open window and tossed it out.

" 'What on earth!' exclaimed Guy . . .

" 'You're referring to that letter? I throw all my letters out of the window. I can't be bothered to toil up and down the stairs every time I post a letter . . .' "

Wodehouse explained that someone or other would always pick them up and post them for him. Two days after Wodehouse had told Bolton of his unusual method of mail delivery, the following incident occurred, as described by Bolton: ". . . Guy heard a timid knocking on his door. He opened it, and a man said, 'Your name "Bolton"?' Guy said it was. 'I've got a letter for you, sir.' Guy put his hand towards his trouser pocket. 'Thank you, sir, but I'm not looking for any tip, I was coming this way.' He felt differently about a beer and Guy poured him one. While he was drinking it, Guy went to the telephone and called Plum.

'I've got your letter,' he said.
Plum said, 'Are you sure it's mine?'
'Yes, of course I'm sure.'
'I only threw it out of the window twenty minutes ago.' "

The second example of an incident that illustrates Wodehouse's open and innocent nature occurred in Hollywood in 1931. Following his year's script-writing contract with Metro-Goldwyn-Mayer, he was interviewed by the Los Angeles Times. While chatting with the reporter before the interview proper began, Wodehouse said with self-deprecating honesty how much he had enjoyed himself in Hollywood, but that his only regret was that he had been paid such vast sums of money ($104,000 in 1930 values; over $1,100,000 in 1981 values) for doing so little work. To Wodehouse's amazement, this casual remark was blazoned across the United States. According to Townend in "Performing Flea", "Before nightfall, Plum was the most talked of man in the United States of America." The bankers who were financing the film industry descended furiously on Hollywood. Film projects were savagely cut. Hollywood, according to Townend, rocked. Wodehouse was bitterly attacked by many of those who had been doing well out of the crazily high spending of the film companies, and he did not return to Hollywood on a further contract until 1936.

A further factor should be mentioned in attempting to evaluate this quality of innocence or trustingness in Wodehouse's character, and that was the unusual and important role played by his wife, Ethel. Wodehouse loved and admired his wife. He relied very greatly upon her. Thelma Cazalet-Keir told me when I was preparing this book: "Although Ethel was very different in character – she was vivacious and gregarious, where he was quiet; she loved parties; he didn't – she was the perfect wife for Plummy. She adored him and admired him. She devoted herself to seeing that his life was just as he wanted it. She took so many burdens off his shoulders so that he could concentrate on his writing. Plummy once told me he knew the exact moment he realised he'd met the girl he would marry. He was picnicking with friends when he developed a dreadful toothache. Ethel, whom he hardly knew then, drove him all the way back to New York. It was a two-hour journey, but in spite of her talkative nature, she never said a single word. She knew just what he needed: to be completely quiet." After they were married, not only did Ethel organise their domestic life, she also handled many of his financial affairs. For example, she negotiated the salaries he was paid of $2,000 and later $2,500 a week in Hollywood. She organised his tax affairs, as already mentioned. The fact that so many mundane problems were lifted from his shoulders by his wife, reinforced Wodehouse's pleasant, trusting and unsuspicious nature.

Within his own world, Wodehouse was conspicuously shrewd and practical. Outside his own world, he was conspicuously not so. He did not even drive a car — following a minor crash on the first and only occasion he ever drove a car, a Darracq he had just bought for £450 in 1906. Wodehouse was not a worldly man. His wife once said of him: "Plummy lives in the moon most of the time."

* * *

It can therefore be said, as definitively as such things ever can be, that the war-time evidence collected by Cussen, combined with the new evidence I uncovered and have set out in this book, prove Wodehouse to have been innocent: innocent of any charge of treason, innocent of cowardice, innocent of Nazi sympathies, innocent of any words or action designed in any way whatsoever to help German war aims, and innocent of any intention whatsoever to do or say anything hostile to his own country or the Allied cause.

Two important questions, however, remain to be answered. First, although Wodehouse was innocent of treachery, was he, in broadcasting, guilty of a culpable error of judgment?

And secondly, why did the British Government, for some 35 years, keep the Wodehouse file an official secret?

To the first question, the answer is complex. My answer would be "No" — having put strong emphasis on the word "culpable" in the question. Looking back with the benefit of hindsight, it is clear that he should not have made the broadcasts. Wodehouse himself admitted it. But, on the evidence available to Wodehouse at the time, and in his circumstances, the question would have appeared in a very different light.

It is certainly true to say that none of Wodehouse's reasons in favour of making the broadcasts was reprehensible. Some were, indeed, admirable — such as the wish to show the outside world that he and his fellow British internees had kept up their courage and cheerfulness during internment by the enemy. But there were other reasons in favour of *not* making the broadcasts, and these Wodehouse did not take into account. In some cases, he could not reasonably be

102

expected to have taken them into account, because he did not know of them – such as the changed British war-time mood – or knew of them only partially, such as the attitude in the neutral United States towards Germany. His decision to broadcast was a mistake but, on balance, it was not a culpable mistake.

Regarding the second question of why successive British Governments kept the Wodehouse file secret for some 35 years, I found two answers. Both reflect discredit on a generation of British politicians and civil servants. The first is contained in the following account of the last application by myself in 1980 – the first having been in 1972 – to the Home Office to see the Wodehouse file. This application, like the previous ones, was refused. I argued against this refusal with the Minister, Lord Belstead, and his advisers. This argument, by exchange of letters and conversations with the Home Office, dragged on for several months. Eventually, I came to the conclusion – although I was never officially told so, in so many words – that there was another Government department in Whitehall that was blocking my application. Which department? Officials said they were not at liberty to discuss it. Lord Belstead and his officials appeared sympathetic and courteous, but said their hands were tied. Their position seemed to me astonishing and untenable, in that even after a knighthood in 1975 had, by implication, cleared Wodehouse's name in one way, the actual details of what he had done were still to be kept officially secret by the British Government, thus implying in another way that guilt in some measure still hung over him.

The situation was disturbingly unsatisfactory. Either Wodehouse was shown by Cussen's evidence to be guilty, in which case the granting of a knighthood was wrong. Or else he was shown to be innocent, in which case the evidence for his innocence should be made public. It is worth recording that when I applied to 1972 to the Prime Minister, Edward Heath, for a knighthood for Wodehouse, and was refused, I had received the clear and strong impression – although it was never said specifically – that the reason for the refusal was some deeply damaging revelation about Wodehouse in the Home Office file.

After further discussions with the Home Office, I began to speculate that somebody else's name was mentioned in a damaging context in the Wodehouse file, and that this was the reason why the file remained secret. I therefore suggested to the Home Office that the other name or names mentioned be blanked out of the original papers, and that I be shown copies of the originals with a blank where the name had been. About a month later, the Home Office agreed to adopt this simple solution.

When I finally read the Wodehouse file, in the Home Office library on 25th June 1980, only one name was blanked out. It was merely the name of the other British internee from Tost, who accompanied Wodehouse to Berlin, and who Wodehouse believed was being released on grounds of age. The name, when I did subsequently learn it by chance, meant nothing to me. That British internee may or may not have been a traitor, although Wodehouse from his own evidence was clearly under the impression that he was not. What is certain is that it would be a case of gross and culpable injustice to Wodehouse if his innocence remained unestablished for some 35 years, and his guilt in some degree presumed, wholly or partly because the British authorities, whether the Home Office or another Government department, were unable to establish the guilt or innocence of another man; or else, omitted later to record in Wodehouse's file that they had subsequently established it, and what its relevance to Wodehouse's actions was.

Yet that one name was apparently a major reason why documents that could have cleared Wodehouse's reputation were kept secret for 35 years. Certainly, no other sufficient reason was apparent once I had read the files. There is nothing in the Wodehouse file, no opinion by a civil servant, no evidence offered by persons interviewed by the security services, no text of a letter between Minister and civil servants, remotely so confidential that such confidentiality should have weighed one feather in the balance against giving public justice to a falsely accused man.

The second reason why the Wodehouse file was kept secret may be found in the predilection of Government departments to stick together, to refuse to divulge information unless compelled to do so, and to cover up their own or colleagues' errors or possible misjudgments, or even mere embarrassments, for as long as possible – a predilection not arising from any deeply sinister motive, and still less from any consciously sustained conspiracy, but arising from an insufficiently strong sense of justice on the part of those civil servants concerned, over the years, and on the part of those politicians who accepted their advice. The normal inclination of Government departments, when in doubt, to maintain the status quo, had triumphed over the requirements of natural justice.

When Wodehouse broadcast from Berlin, it was a Government department, the Ministry of Information, then under Duff Cooper, that led the campaign of vilification against him. The Ministry was strongly advised not to attack Wodehouse by the Governors of the B.B.C. But Duff Cooper over-ruled the Governors. He personally insisted on the B.B.C. broadcasting Cassandra's attack, as his letter to The Times on 22nd July 1941, already quoted, clearly states.

Although Duff Cooper's motives were good, the means were bad. The Ministry, in its sponsorship of Cassandra's broadcast, contravened the very values for which the Allies were fighting. Furthermore, whatever justification there may have been for Duff Cooper and Cassandra in 1941, there can be no justification for later Ministers and civil servants allowing what official Government files showed to be an injustice against Wodehouse, to remain unrighted.

The wrong against Wodehouse was fostered by one Government department in 1941, and for some 35 years after the end of the Second World War other Government departments were instrumental in concealing facts which would have revealed that a wrong had been done.

The workings of the political and bureaucratic machine perpetrated, and for 35 years perpetuated, a grave injustice upon Wodehouse, which he took to his grave.

Appendix One

The Berlin Broadcasts
[Official transcripts made by the German Foreign Office]

The First Berlin Broadcast

This is the German Shortwave Station. Here in our studio in Berlin tonight is Mr. P. G. Wodehouse, the well known father [sic] of the inimitable Jeeves, of Bertie Worcester [sic], Lord Emsworth, Mr. Mulliner, and other delightful persons. Mr. Wodehouse has been in Germany for almost a year since German troops occupied his residence in Northern France. During that time he has finished a new novel which, I understand, is on its way to the United States for publication, and started with another one. We felt that his American readers might be interested to hear from Mr. Wodehouse, so we have invited him to this microphone to tell you in his own words how it all happened.

Mr. Wodehouse:

It is just possible that my listeners may seem to detect in this little talk of mine a slight goofiness, a certain disposition to ramble in my remarks. If so, the matter, as Bertie Wooster would say, is susceptible of a ready explanation. I have just emerged into the outer world after forty-nine weeks of Civil Internment in a German internment camp and the effects have not entirely worn off. I have not yet quite recovered that perfect mental balance for which in the past I was so admired by one and all.

It's coming back, mind you. Look me up a couple of weeks from now, and you'll be surprised. But just at the moment I feel slightly screwy and inclined to pause at intervals in order to cut out paper dolls and stick straws in my hair – or such of my hair as I still have.

This, no doubt, is always the effect of prolonged internment, and since July the twenty-first, 1940, I have been spending my time in a series of Ilags. An Ilag must not be confused with an Offlag or a Stalag. An Offlag is where captured officers go. A stalag is reserved for the rank and file. The Civil Internee gets the Ilag – and how he loves it!

Since I went into business for myself as an internee, I have been in no fewer than four Ilags – some more Ilaggy than others, others less Ilaggy than some. First, they put us in a prison, then in a barracks, then in a fortress. Then they took a look at me and the rest of the boys on parade one day, and got the right idea at last. They sent us off to the local lunatic asylum at Tost in Upper Silesia, and there I have been for the last forty-two weeks.

It has been in many ways quite an agreeable experience. There is a good deal to be said for internment. It keeps you out of the saloons and gives you time to catch up with your reading. You also get a lot of sleep. The chief drawback is that it means your being away from home a good deal. It is not pleasant to think that by the time I see my Pekinese again, she will have completely forgotten me and will bite me to the bone – her invariable practice with strangers. And I feel that when I rejoin my wife, I had better take along a letter of introduction, just to be on the safe side.

Young men, starting out in life, have often asked me 'How can I become an Internee?' Well, there are several methods. My own was to buy a villa in Le Touquet on the coast of France and stay there till the Germans came along. This is probably the best and simplest system. You buy the villa and the Germans do the rest.

At the time of their arrival, I would have been just as pleased if they had not rolled up. But they did not see it that way, and on May the twenty-second along they came, – some on motor cycles, some on foot, but all evidently prepared to spend a long week-end.

The whole thing was very peaceful and orderly. Le Touquet has the advantage of being a sort of backwater, off the line of march. Your tendency, if you are an army making for the coast, is to carry on along the main road to Boulogne, and not to take the first turning to the left when you reach Étaples. So the proceedings were not marred by any vulgar brawling. All that happened, as far as I was concerned, was that I was strolling on the lawn with my wife one morning, when she lowered her voice and said "Don't look now, but there comes the German army". And there they were, a fine body of men, rather prettily dressed in green, carrying machine guns.

One's reactions on suddenly finding oneself surrounded by the armed strength of a hostile power are rather interesting. There is a sense of strain. The first time you see a German soldier over your garden fence, your impulse is to jump ten feet straight up into the air, and you do so. About a week later, you find that you are only jumping five feet. And then, after you have been living with him in a small village for two months, you inevitably begin to fraternize and to wish that you had learned German at school instead of Latin and Greek. All the German I know is 'Es ist schönes Wetter', I was a spent force, and we used to take out the rest of the interview in beaming at one another.

I had a great opportunity of brushing up my beaming during those two months. My villa stands in the centre of a circle of houses, each of which was occupied by German officers, who would come around at intervals to take a look at things, and the garden next door was full of Labour Corps boys. It was with these that one really got together. There was scarcely an evening when two or three of them did not drop in for a bath at my house and a beaming party on the porch afterwards.

And so, day by day, all through June and July, our quiet, happy life continued, with not a jarring incident to mar the serenity. Well, yes, perhaps one or two. One day, an official-looking gentleman with none of the Labour Corps geniality came along and said he wanted my car. Also my radio. And in addition my bicycle. That was what got under the skin. I could do without the car, and I had never much liked the radio, but I loved that bicycle. I looked him right in the eye and said 'Es ist schönes Wetter' – and I said it nastily. I meant it to sting. And what did he say? He didn't say anything. What could we have said? P.S. He got the bicycle.

But these were small things, scarcely causing a ripple on the placid stream of life in the occupied areas. A perfect atmosphere of peace and goodwill continued to prevail. Except for the fact that I was not allowed out of my garden after nine at night, my movements were not restricted. Quite soon I had become sufficiently nonchalant to resume the writing o˄ the novel which the arrival of the soldiery had interrupted. And then the order went out that all British subjects had got to report each morning at twelve o'clock at the Kommandantur down in Paris Plage.

As Paris Plage was three miles away, and they had pinched my bicycle, this was a nuisance. But I should have had nothing to complain of, if the thing had stopped there. But unfortunately it didn't. One lovely Sunday morning, as I was rounding into the straight and heading for the door of the Kommandantur, I saw one of our little group coming along with a suitcase in his hand.

This didn't look so good. I was conscious of a nameless fear. Wodehouse, old sport, I said to myself, this begins to look like a sticky day. And a few moments later my apprehensions were fulfilled. Arriving at the Kommandantur, I found everything in a state of bustle and excitement. I said "Es ist schones wetter" once or twice, but nobody took any notice. And presently the interpreter stepped forward and announced that we were all going to be interned.

It was a pretty nasty shock, coming without warning out of a blue sky like that, and it is not too much to say that for an instant the old maestro shook like a badly set blancmange. Many years ago, at a party which had started to get a bit rough, somebody once hit me on the bridge of the nose with an order of planked steak. As I had felt then, so did I feel now. That same sensation of standing in a rocking and disintegrating world.

I didn't realize at the time how such luckier I was than a great many other victims of the drag-net. All over France during that Sunday, British citizens were being picked up and taken away without being given time to pack, and for a week those in Boulogne had been living in what they stood up in at the Petit Vitesse railroad station. For some reason, Le Touquet was given a substantial break. We were allowed to go home and put a few things together, and as my home was three miles away, I was actually sent there in a car.

The soldier who escorted me was unfortunately not one of those leisurely souls who believe in taking time over one's packing. My idea had been to have a cold bath and a change and a bite to eat, and then to light a pipe and sit down and muse for a while, making notes of what to take with me and what could be left behind. His seemed to be that five minutes was ample. Eventually we compromised on ten.

I would like my biographers to make careful note of the fact that the first thing that occurred to me was that here at last was my chance to buckle down and read the complete works of William Shakespeare. It was a thing I had been meaning to do any time these last forty years, but somehow, as soon as I had got – say, Hamlet and Macbeth under my belt and was preparing to read the stuffing out of Henry the Sixth, parts one, two and three, something like the Murglow Manor Mystery would catch my eye and I would weaken.

I didn't know what interment implied – it might be for years or it might be for ever – or it might be a mere matter of weeks – but the whole situation seemed to point to the complete works of William Shakespeare, so in they went. I am happy to say that I am now crammed with Shakespeare to the brim, so, whatever else internment has done for me, I am at any rate that much ahead of the game.

It was a pang to leave my novel behind, I had only five more chapters of it to do. But space, as Jeeves would have pointed out, was of the essence, and it had to go, and is now somewhere in France. I am hoping to run into it again one of these days, for it was a nice little novel and we had some great times together.

I wonder what my listeners would have packed in my place – always remembering that there was a German soldier standing behind me all the time, shouting "Schnell" or words to that effect. I had to think quick. Eventually what I crammed in were tobacco, pencils, scribbling blocks, chocolate, biscuits, a pair of trousers, a pair of shoes, some shirts and a sock or two. My wife wanted to add a pound of butter, but I fought her off. There are practically no limits to what a pound of butter can do in warm weather in a small suitcase. If I was going to read the complete works of William Shakespeare, I preferred them unbuttered.

In the end, the only thing of importance I left behind was my passport, which was the thing I ought to have packed first. The young internee is always being asked for his passport, and if he hasn't got it, the authorities tend to look squiggle-eyes and to ask nasty questions. I had never fully realized what class distinctions were till I became an internee without a passport, thus achieving a social position somewhere in between a minor gangster and a wharf rat.

Having closed the suitcase and said goodbye to my wife and the junior dog, and foiled the attempt of the senior dog to muscle into the car and accompany me into captivity, I returned to the Kommandantur. And presently, with the rest of the gang, numbering twelve in all, I drove in a motor omnibus for an unknown destination.

That is one of the drawbacks to travelling, when you are an internee. Your destination always is unknown. It is unsettling, when you start out, not to be sure whether you are going half way across Europe or just to the next town. Actually, we were headed for Loos, a suburb of Lille, a distance of about a hundred miles. What with stopping at various points along the road to pick up other foundation members, it took us eight hours.

An internee's enjoyment of such a journey depends very largely on the mental attitude of the sergeant in charge. Ours turned out to be a genial soul, who gave us cigarettes and let us get off and buy red wine at all stops, infusing the whole thing [with] a pleasant atmosphere of the school treat. This was increased by the fact that we all knew each other pretty intimately and had hobnobbed on other occasions. Three of us were from the golf club – Arthur Grant, the Pro., Jeff, the starter, and Max, the caddie master. Algy, of Algy's bar in the Rue St. Jean, was there, and Alfred, of Alfred's bar in the Rue de Paris. And the rest, like Charlie Webb and Bill Illidge, who ran garages, were all well-known Paris Plage figures. The thing was, therefore, practically a feast of reason and a flow of soul.

Nevertheless as the evening shadows began to fall and the effects of the red wine to wear off, we were conscious of a certain sinking feeling. We felt very far from our snug homes and not at all sure that we liked the shape of things to come.

As to what exactly *was* the shape of things to come, nobody seemed to know. But the general sentiment that prevailed was one of uneasiness. We feared the worst.

Nor were we greatly encouraged, when, having passed through Lille, we turned down a side lane and came through pleasant fields and under spreading trees to a forbidding-looking building which was only too obviously the local hoose-gow or calaboose. A nasty-looking man in the uniform of the French provincial police flung wide the gates and we rolled through.

Next week, – the Rover Boys in Loos Prison.

That was Mr. Wodehouse in the first broadcast of a series of weekly talks which he will give from this station.

The Second Berlin Broadcast

This is the German Shortwave Station. Here in our studio in Berlin tonight is Mr. P. G. Wodehouse, the well known father [sic] of Jeeves, of Bertie Wooster, Lord Emsworth, Mr. Mulliner, and other delightful persons. Mr. Wodehouse has been in Germany for almost a year since German troops occupied his residence in Northern France. During that time he has finished a new novel which, I understand, is on its way to the United States for publication and started with another one. We felt that his American readers might be interested to hear Mr. Wodehouse continuing his story.

P. G. Wodehouse:

I broke off my Odyssey of the internees of Le Touquet last week, if you remember, with our little band of pilgrims entering Loos Prison. Owing to having led a blameless life since infancy, I had never seen the interior of a calaboose before, and directly I set eyes on the official in the front office, I

111

regretted that I was doing so now. There are moments, as we pass through life, when we gaze into a stranger's face and say to ourselves 'I have met a friend'. This was not one of those occasions. There is probably nobody in the world less elfin than a French prison official, and the one now twirling a Grover Whalen moustache at me looked like something out of a film about Devil's Island.

Still, an author never quite gives up hope, and I think there was just a faint idea at the back of my mind that mine host, on hearing my name, would start to his feet with a cry of 'Quoi? Monsieur Vodeouse? Embrassez-moi, maitre!' and offer me his bed for the night, adding that he had long been one of my warmest admirers and would I give his little daughter my autograph.

Nothing like that happened. He just twirled the moustache again, entered my name in a large book, – or, rather, he put down 'Widhorse', the silly son of a bachelor, – and motioned to the bashi-bazouks to lead me to my cell. Or, as it turned out, the communal cell of myself, Algy of Algy's Bar and Mr. Cartmell, our courteous and popular piano-tuner. For in those piping times of war – I don't know how it is on ordinary occasions – Loos Prison was bedding out its guests three to the room.

It was now getting on for ten o'clock at night, and it was this, I discovered later, that saved us a lot of unpleasantness. Round about the hour of ten, the French prison official tends to slacken up a bit. He likes to get into something loose and relax over a good book, and this makes him go through the motions of housing a batch of prisoners quickly and perfunctorily. When I got out into the exercise yard next morning, and met some of the men who had been in the place for a week, I found that they, on arrival, had been stood with their faces to the wall, stripped to their B.V.D.s, deprived of all their belongings and generally made to feel like so many imprisoned pieces of cheese. All they did to us was take away our knives and money and leave us.

Cells in French prisons are built for privacy. Where in the gaols of America there are bars, here you have only a wall with an iron-studded door in it. You go in, and this door is slammed and locked behind you, and you find yourself in a snug little apartment measuring about twelve feet by eight. At the far end is a window and under it a bed. Against the opposite wall to the bed there stands a small table and – chained to it – a chair of the type designed for the use of Singer's Midgets. In the corner by the door is a faucet with a basin beneath it, and beyond this what Chic Sale would call a 'family one-holer'. The only pictures on the walls, which are of white-washed stone, are those drawn from time to time by French convicts – boldly executed pencil sketches very much in the vein which you would expect from French convicts.

Cartmell being the senior member of our trio, we gave him the bed, and Algy and I turned in on the floor. It was the first time I had tried dossing on a thin mattress on a granite floor, but we Wodehouses are tough stuff, and it was not long before the tired eyelids closed in sleep. My last waking thought, I remember, was that, while this was a hell of a thing to have happened to a respectable old gentleman in his declining years, it was all pretty darned interesting and that I could hardly wait to see what the morrow would bring forth.

What the morrow brought forth, at seven sharp, was a rattling of keys and the opening of a small panel in the door, through which were thrust three tin mugs containing a thin and lukewarm soup and three loaves of bread, a dark sepia in color. This, one gathered, was breakfast, and the problem arose of how to play our part in the festivities. The soup was all right. One could manage that. You just took a swallow, and then another swallow – to see if it had really tasted as bad as it had seemed to the first time, and before you knew where you were, it had gone. But how, not having knives, we were to deal with the bread presented a greater test of our ingenuity. Biting bits off it was not a practical proposition for my companions, whose teeth were not of the best: and it was no good hammering it on the edge of the table, because it simply splintered the woodwork. But there is always a way of getting around life's little difficulties, if you give your mind to it. I became bread-biter to the community, and I think I gave satisfaction. At any rate, I got the stuff apart.

At eight-thirty, the key rattled again, and we were let out for air, recreation and exercise. That is to say, we were taken into an enclosure with high brick walls, partially open to the sky, and allowed to stand there for half an hour.

There was nothing much we could do except stand, for the enclosure – constructed, apparently, by an architect who had seen the Black Hole of Calcutta and admired it – was about twelve yards long, six yards wide at the broad end, tapering off to two yards wide at the narrow end, and we had to share it with the occupants of other cells. No chance, I mean, of getting up an informal football game or a truck-meet or anything like that.

Having stood for thirty minutes, we returned to our cells, greatly refreshed, and remained there for the next twenty-three and a half hours. At twelve, we got some soup, and at five some more soup. Different kinds of soup, of course. Into the twelve o'clock ration a cabbage had been dipped – hastily, by a cook who didn't like getting his hands wet, and in the other there was a bean, actually floating about, visible to the naked eye.

Next day, the key rattled in the lock at seven, and we got soup, and at eight-thirty our scamper in the great open spaces, followed by soup at twelve and more soup at five. The day after than, the key rattled in the lock at seven, and we . . . But you get the idea. What you would call a healthy, regular life, giving a man plenty of leisure for reading the Complete Works of William Shakespeare – as, if you remember, I had resolved to do.

Apart from Shakespeare, who is unquestionably a writer who takes you away from it all, what made existence tolerable was the window. I had always understood that prison cells had small windows of ground glass, placed high up near the ceiling, but ours was a spacious affair of about five feet by four, and you could open it wide and even, by standing on the bed, get a glimpse from it of a vegetable garden and fields beyond. And the air that came through it was invaluable in keeping our cell smell within reasonable bounds.

113

The cell smell is a great feature of all French prisons. Ours in Number Forty-Four at Loos was one of those fine, broad-shouldered, up-and-coming young smells which stand on both feet and look the world in the eye. We became very fond and proud of it, championing it hotly against other prisoners who claimed that theirs had more authority and bouquet, and when the first German officer to enter our little sanctum rocked back on his heels and staggered out backwards, we took it as almost a personal compliment. It was like hearing a tribute paid to an old friend.

Nevertheless, in spite of the interest of hobnobbing with our smell, we found time hang a little heavy on our hands. I was all right. I had my Complete Works of William Shakespeare. But Algy had no drinks to mix, and Cartmell no pianos to tune. And a piano-tuner suddenly deprived of pianos is like a tiger whose medical adviser has put it on a vegetarian diet. Cartmell used to talk to us of pianos he had tuned in the past, and sometimes he would speak easily and well of pianos he hoped to tune in the future, but it was not the same. You could see that what the man wanted was a piano *now*. Either that, or something to take his mind off the thing.

It was on the fourth morning, accordingly, that we addressed a petition to the German Kommandant, pointing out that, as we were civil internees, not convicts, there was surely no need for all this Ballad of Reading Gaol stuff, and asking if it would not be possible to inject a little more variety into our lives.

This appeal to Caesar worked like magic. Apparently the Kommandant had not had a notion that we were being treated as we were – the French had thought it up all by themselves – and he exploded like a bomb. We could hear distant reverberations of his wrath echoing along the corridors, and presently there came the old, familiar rattle of keys, and pallid warders opened the doors and informed us that from now on we were at liberty to roam about the prison at will.

Everything is relative – as somebody once said – probably Shakespeare in his Complete Works – and I cannot remember when I have felt such a glorious sense of freedom as when I strolled out of my cell, leaving the door open behind me, and started to saunter up and down outside.

And, even if it shows a vindictive spirit, I must confess that the pleasure was increased by the sight of the horror and anguish on the faces of the prison personnel. If there is one man who is a stickler for tradition and etiquette, for what is done and what is not done, it is the French prison warder, and here were tradition and etiquette being chucked straight into the ash-can, and nothing to be done about it. I suppose their feelings were rather what those of a golf professional would be, if he had to submit to seeing people dancing on his putting greens in high-heeled shoes.

In the end, we got quite sorry for the poor chaps, and relented to the extent of allowing them to lock us in for the night. It was pathetic to see how they brightened up at this concession. It paved the way to an understanding, and before we left the place we had come to be on quite friendly terms.

One of them actually unbent to the extent of showing us the condemned cell – much as the host at a country house takes his guest round the stables.

Our great topic of conversation, as we strolled about the corridors, was, of course, where we were going from here, and when. For we could not believe that Loos Prison was anything but a temporary resting place. And we were right. A week after we had arrived, we were told to line up in the corridor, and presently the Kommandant appeared and informed us that, after our papers had been examined, we were to pack and be ready to leave.

Men of sixty and over, he added, would be released and sent home, so these lucky stiffs went and stood to one side in a row, looking like a beauty chorus. On the strength of being fifty-eight and three-quarters, I attempted to join them, but was headed back. Fifty-eight and three-quarters was good, I was given to understand, but not good enough.

I did not brood about this much, however, for it has just occurred to me that, having left my passport behind, I might quite easily have to stay on after the others had gone wherever they were going. Fortunately, I had twelve stout fellows from Le Touquet to testify to my identity and respectability, and they all lined up beside me and did their stuff. The Kommandant was plainly staggered by this cloud of witnesses, and in the end I just got under the wire.

This was on the Saturday evening, and far into the night the place buzzed with speculation. I don't know who first started the rumor that we were going to the barracks at Liége, but he turned out to be quite right. That was where we were headed for, and at eleven o'clock next morning we were given our mid-day soup and hustled out and dumped into vans and driven to the station.

One would have supposed from the atmosphere of breathless bustle that the train was scheduled to pull out at about eleven-thirty, but this was not the case. Our Kommandant was a careful man. I think he must once have missed an important train, and it preyed on his mind. At any rate, he got us there at eleven-forty a.m. and the journey actually started at eight o'clock in the evening. I can picture the interview between him and the sergeant when the latter returned. 'Did those boys make that train?' . . . 'Yes, sir, – by eight hours and twenty minutes.'. . . 'Whew! Close thing. Mustn't run it so fine another time.'

As a matter of fact, all through my period of internment I noticed this tendency on the part of the Germans to start our little expeditions off with a whoop and a rush and then sort of lose interest. It reminded me of Hollywood. When you are engaged to work at Hollywood, you get a cable saying that it is absolutely vital that you be there by ten o'clock on the morning of June the first. Ten-five will be too late, and as for getting there on June the second, that means ruin to the industry. So you rush about and leap into aeroplanes, and at ten o'clock on June the first you are at the studio, being told that you cannot see your employer now, as he has gone to Palm Springs. Nothing happens after this till October the twentieth, when you are given an assignment and told that every moment is precious.

It is the same with the Germans in this matter of making trains. They like to leave a margin.

Summing up my experience as a gaol-bird, I would say that a prison is all right for a visit, but I wouldn't live there, if you gave me the place. On my part, at any rate, there was no moaning at the bar when I left Loos. I was glad to go. The last I saw of the old Alma Mater was the warder closing the door of the van and standing back with the French equivalent of 'Right away'.

He said 'Au revoir' to me – which I thought a little tactless.

That was Mr. Wodehouse in the second broadcast of a series of weekly talks which he will give from this station.

The Third Berlin Broadcast

The last instalment of my serial narrative entitled 'How To Be An Internee And Like It' ended, you may remember, with our band of pilgrims catching the train from Lille by the skin of our teeth, – that is to say, with a bare eight hours and twenty minutes to spare. The next thing that happened was the journey to Liége.

One drawback to being an internee is that, when you move from spot to spot, you have to do it in company with eight hundred other men. This precludes anything in the nature of travel de luxe. We made the twenty-four hour trip in a train consisting of those 'Quarante Hommes, Huit Chevaux' things – in other words, cattle trucks. I had sometimes seen them on sidings on French railroads in times of peace, and had wondered what it would be like to be one of the Quarante Hommes. I now found out, and the answer is that it is pretty darned awful. Eight horses might manage to make themselves fairly comfortable in one of these cross-country loose-boxes, but forty men are cramped. Every time I stretched my legs, I kicked a human soul. This would not have mattered so much, but every time the human souls stretched *their* legs, they kicked *me*. The only pleasant recollection I have of that journey is the time when we were let out for ten minutes on the banks of the Meuse.

Arriving at Liége, and climbing the hill to the barracks, we found an atmosphere of unpreparedness. Germany at that time was like the old woman who lived in a shoe. She had so many adopted children that she didn't know what to do with them. As regards our little lot, I had a feeling that she did not really want us, but didn't like to throw us away.

The arrangements for our reception at Liége seemed incomplete. It was as if one had got to a party much too early. Here, for instance, were eight hundred men who were going to live mostly on soup – and though the authorities knew where to lay their hands on some soup all right, nothing had been provided to put it in

116

And eight hundred internees can't just go to the cauldron and lap. For one thing, they would burn their tongues, and for another the quick swallowers would get more than their fair share. The situation was one that called for quick thinking, and it was due to our own resourcefulness that the problem was solved. At the back of the barrack yard there was an enormous rubbish heap, into which Belgian soldiers through the ages had been dumping old mess tins, old cans, cups with bits chipped off them, bottles, kettles and containers for motor oil. We dug these out, gave them a wash and brush up, and there we were. I had the good fortune to secure one of the motor oil containers. It added to the taste of the soup just that little something that the others hadn't got.

Liége bore the same resemblance to a regular prison camp, like the one we were eventually to settle down in at Tost, which a rough scenario does to a finished novel. There was a sort of rudimentary organization – that is to say, we were divided into dormitories, each with a Room Warden – but when I think of Tost, with its Camp Captain, Camp Adjutants, Camp Committees and so on, Liége seems very primitive. It was also extraordinarily dirty, as are most places which have recently been occupied by Belgian soldiers. A Belgian soldier doesn't consider home is home, unless he can write his name in the alluvial deposits on the floor.

We spent a week at Liége, and, looking back, I can hardly believe that our stay there lasted only a mere seven days. This is probably due to the fact that there was practically nothing to do but stand around. We shared the barracks with a number of French military prisoners, and as we were not allowed to mix with them, we had to confine ourselves to a smallish section of the barrack yard. There was not room to do anything much except stand, so we stood. I totted up one day the amount of standing I had done between reveille and lights out – including parades and queuing up for meals – and it amounted to nearly six hours. The only time we were not standing was when we were lying on our beds in the afternoon. For we had beds at Liége, which was about the only improvement on the dear old prison we had left.

Parades took place at eight in the morning and eight in the evening, and as far as they were concerned I did not object to having to stand each time for fifty minutes or so, for they provided solid entertainment for the thoughtful mind. You might think that fifty minutes was a long time for eight hundred men to get themselves counted, but you would have understood, if you had seen us in action. I don't know why it was, but we could never get the knack of parading. We meant well, but we just didn't seem able to click.

The proceedings would start with the Sergeant telling us to form fives. This order having been passed along the line by the linguists who understood German, we would nod intelligently and form fours, then threes, then sixes. And when eventually, just in time to save the Sergeant from having a nervous breakdown, we managed to get into fives, was this the end? No, sir. It was not an end, but a beginning. What happened then was that Old Bill in Row Forty-Two would catch sight of Old George in Row Twenty-Three and shuffle across to have a chat with him, a cigarette hanging from his lower lip.

Time marches on. Presently, Old Bill, having heard all Old George has to say about the European situation, decides to shuffle back – only to find that his place has been filled up, like a hole by the tide. This puzzles him for a moment, but he soon sees what to do. He forms up as the seventh man of a row, just behind Old Percy, who has been chatting with Old Fred and has just come back and lined up as Number Six.

A Corporal with sheep-dog blood in him now comes into the picture. He cuts Bill and Percy out of the flock and chivvies them around for a while, and after a good deal of shouting the ranks are apparently in order once more.

But is *this* the end? Again no. The Sergeant, the Corporal, and a French soldier interpreter now walk the length of the ranks, counting. They then step aside and go into a sort of football huddle. A long delay. Something is wrong. The word goes round that we are one short, and the missing man is believed to be Old Joe. We discuss this with growing interest. Has Old Joe escaped? Maybe the jailer's daughter smuggled him in a file in a meat pie.

No. Here comes Old Joe, sauntering along with a pipe in his mouth and eyeing us in an indulgent sort of way, as who should say 'Hullo, boys. Playing soldiers, eh? May *I* join in?' He is thoroughly cursed – in German by the Sergeant, in French by the interpreter and in English by us – and takes his place in the parade.

As practically the whole of the personnel has left the ranks to cluster round and listen to the Sergeant talking to Old Joe, it is now necessary to count us again. This is done, and there is another conference. This time, in some mysterious way, we have become six short, and a discouraged feeling grows among us. It looks as if we were losing ground.

A Priest now steps forward. He is a kind of liaison officer between us and the Germans. He asks 'Have the six men who came from Ghent registered at the bureau?' But Lord Peter Wimsey is not going to solve the mystery as easily as that. Apparently they have, and there follows another huddle. Then all Room Wardens are invited to join the conference, and it is announced that we are to return to our dormitories, where the Room Wardens will check up their men and assemble them.

My dormitory – Fifty-Two B – goes to the length of getting a large sheet of cardboard and writing on it in chalk the words 'Zwansig Manner, Stimmt' – which our linguist assures us means 'Twenty Men, All Present', and when the whistle blows again for the renewal of the parade, I hold this in front of me like a London sandwich-man. It doesn't get a smile from Teacher, which is disappointing, but this is perhaps not [to] be wondered at, for he is very busy trying to count us again in our peculiar formation. For Old Bill has once more strolled off to Old George and has got into an argument with him about whether yesterday's coffee tasted more strongly of gasoline than today's. Bill thinks Yes – George isn't so sure.

They are chased back by the Corporal, now baying like a bloodhound, and there is another conference. We are now five short. The situation seems to be at a deadlock, with no hope of ever finding a formula, when some bright person – Monsieur Poirot, perhaps – says, 'How about the men in the hospital?' These prove to be five in number, and we are dismissed. We have spent a pleasant and instructive fifty minutes, and learned much about our fellow men.

Much the same thing happens when we line up at seven a.m. for breakfast, and at eleven-thirty and seven p.m. for lunch and supper – except that here we are in a movement, and so can express ourselves better. For if we are a little weak on keeping the ranks when standing still, we go all haywire when walking, and not many steps are required to turn us into something like a mob charging out of a burning building.

Meals are served from large cauldrons outside the cookhouse door at the far end of the barrack yard, and the Corporal, not with very much hope in his voice, for he has already seen us in action, tells us to form fours. We do so, and for a while it looks as if the thing were really going to be a success this time. Then it suddenly occurs to Old Bill, Old George, Old Joe and Old Percy, together with perhaps a hundred and twenty of their fellow internees, that by leaving their places at the tail of the procession and running round and joining the front row, they will get theirs quicker. They immediately proceed to do this, and are at once followed by about eighty other rapid thinkers, who have divined their thought-processes and have come to the conclusion that the idea is a good one. Twenty minutes later, a white-haired Corporal with deep furrows in his forehead has restored the formation into fours, and we start again.

On a good morning – I mean a morning when Old Bill and his associates were in their best form – it would take three-quarters of an hour for the last in line to reach the cookhouse, and one used to wonder what it would be like on a rainy day.

Fortunately, the rainy day never came. The weather was still fine when, a week from our arrival, we were loaded into vans and driven to the station, our destination being the Citadel of Huy, about twenty-five miles away – another Belgian army center.

If somebody were to ask me whose quarters I would prefer to take over – those of French convicts or Belgian soldiers, I would find it hard to say. French convicts draw pictures on the walls of their cells which bring the blush of shame to the cheek of modesty, but they are fairly tidy in their habits – whereas Belgian soldiers, as I have mentioned before, make lots of work for their successors. Without wishing to be indelicate, I may say that, until you have helped to clean out a Belgian soldiers' latrine, you ain't seen nuttin'.

It was my stay at Liège, and subsequently at the Citadel of Huy, that gave me that wholesome loathing for Belgians which is the hall-mark of the discriminating man. If I never see anything Belgian again in this world, it will be all right with me.

The Fourth Berlin Broadcast

Here in our studio in Berlin tonight is Mr. P. G. Wodehouse the well known father [sic] of Jeeves, of Bertie Wooster, Lord Emsworth, Mr. Mulliner, and other delightful persons. We felt that his American readers might be interested to hear Mr. Wodehouse continuing his story.

Here is Mr. Wodehouse.

Before beginning my talk tonight – the fourth of a series of five dealing with the five phases of my internment – I should like to say another few words on another subject.

The Press and Public of England seem to have jumped to the conclusion that I have been in some way bribed or intimidated into making these broadcasts. This is not the case.

I did not 'make a bargain', as they put it, and buy my release by agreeing to speak over the radio. I was released because I am sixty years old – or shall be in October. The fact that I was free a few months before that date was due to the efforts of my friends. As I pointed out in my second talk, if I had been sixty when I was interned, I should have been released at the end of the first week.

My reason for broadcasting was a simple one. In the course of my period of internment I received hundreds of letters of sympathy from American readers of my books, who were strangers to me, and I was naturally anxious to let them know how I had got on.

Under existing conditions, it was impossible to answer these letters, – and I did not want to be so ungrateful and ungracious as to seem to be ignoring them, and the radio suggested itself as a solution.

I will now go on to my experiences in the Citadel of Huy – the last of the places where we were lodged before we finally settled at Tost, in Upper Silesia.

In putting [together] these talks on How To Be An Internee Without Previous Training, I find myself confronted by the difficulty of deciding what aspects of my daily life, when in custody, will have entertainment value for listeners.

When the war is over and I have my grandchildren as an audience, this problem, of course, will not arise. The unfortunate little blighters will get the whole thing, night after night, without cuts. But now I feel that a certain process of selection is necessary. A good deal that seems to an internee thrilling and important is so only to himself. Would it interest you, for instance, to hear that it took us four hours to do the twenty-five mile journey from Liége to Huy, and that there were moments during the walk up the mountain-side when the old boy thought he was going to expire? No, I thought not.

It is for this reason that I propose to pass fairly lightly over my five weeks' stay at Huy. Don't let that name confuse you, by the way. It is spelled H-u-y, and in any other country but Belgium would be pronounced Hoo-ey. So remember that, when I say Huy, I don't mean 'we' – I mean Huy.

The Citadel of Huy is one of those show places they charge you two francs to go into in times of peace. I believe it was actually built in the time of the Napoleonic wars, but its atmosphere is purely mediaeval. It looks down on the River Meuse from the summit of a mountain – the sort of mountain Gutzon Borglum would love to carve pictures on – and it is one of those places where, once you're in, you're in. Its walls are fourteen feet thick, and the corridors are lighted by bays, in which are narrow slits of windows. It is through these, if you are a married man with a wife living in Belgium, that you shout to her when she comes to visit you. She stands on the slope below, as high up as she can get, and shouts to *you*. Neither can see the other, and the whole thing is like something out of Il Trovatore.

The only place in the building from which it is possible to get a view of somebody down below is the window of what afterwards became the canteen room. Men would rush in there and fling themselves through the window and lie face down on the broad sill. It was startling till one got used to it, and one never quite lost the fear that they would lose their heads and jump. But this lying on sills was forbidden later, as were most things at Huy, where the slogan seemed to be 'Go and see what the internees are doing, and tell them they mustn't'. I remember an extra parade being called, so that we might be informed that stealing was forbidden. This hit us very hard.

These extra parades were a great feature of life at Huy, for our Kommandant seemed to have a passion for them.

Mind you, I can find excuses for him. If I had been in his place, I would have ordered extra parades myself. His headquarters were down in the town, and there was no road connecting the Citadel with the outer world – just a steep, winding path. So that, when he came to visit us, he had to walk. He was a fat, short-legged man in the middle sixties, and walking up steep, winding paths does something to fat, short-legged men who are not as young as they were. Duty called him now and then to march up the hill and to march down again, but nothing was going to make him like it.

I picture him starting out, full of loving kindness – all sweetness and light, as it were – and gradually becoming more and more soured as he plodded along. So that when he eventually came to journey's end with a crick in the back and the old dogs feeling as if they were about to burst like shrapnel, and saw us loafing around at our ease, the sight was too much for him and he just reached for his whistle and blew it for an extra parade.

Extra parades were also called two or three times a day by the Sergeant, when there was any announcement to be made. At Tost we had a notice-board, on which camp orders were posted each day, but this ingenious system had not occurred to anyone at Huy. The only way they could think

121

of there of establishing communication between the front office and the internees was to call a parade. Three whistles would blow, and we would assemble in the yard, and after a long interval devoted to getting into some sort of formation we would be informed that there was a parcel for Omer – or that we must shave daily – or that we must not smoke on parade – or that we must not keep our hands in our pockets on parade – or that we might buy playing cards – (and next day that we might *not* buy playing cards) – or that boys must not cluster round the guard-room trying to scrounge food from the soldiers – or that there was a parcel for Omer.

I remember once, in the days when I used to write musical comedies, a chorus girl complaining to me with some bitterness that if a carpenter had to drive a nail into a flat, the management would be sure to call a chorus rehearsal to watch him do it, and I could now understand just how she had felt. I don't know anything that brings the grimness of life home to one more than hearing three whistles blow just as you are in the middle of a bath – and leaping into your clothes without drying – and lining up in the yard and waiting twenty minutes at attention – and then being informed that there is a parcel for Omer.

It was not that we had anything against Omer. We all liked him – and never better than when he had just had a parcel, but what embittered us was that there was never a parcel for anyone else. He happened to have been interned right on the spot where all his friends and admirers lived, while the rest of us were far from home and had not yet been able to get in touch with our wives. It was that that made these first weeks of internment such a nightmare. Not receiving parcels was merely a side-issue. It would have been nice to have had some, but we could do without them. But we did wish that we could have got some information as to how our wives were getting on. It was only later at Tost, that we began to receive letters and to be able to write them.

The few letters which did trickle in to Huy from time to time were regarded by the authorities with strong suspicion. After a parade had been called, for us to watch them given out, their recipients would be allowed a couple of minutes to read them – then they would have to hand them back to the Corporal, who tore them up. And when Omer got one of his parcels, its contents would all be opened before he was permitted to take them away – from the first can of sardines to the last bit of chocolate. I believe this was due entirely to the men who, at the end of the last war, wrote books telling how clever they had been at escaping from German prison camps by means of codes sent by letter and compasses and so on enclosed in potted meat. They meant no harm, but they certainly made it tough for us.

'Tough' is the adjective I would use to describe the whole of those five weeks at Huy. The first novelty of internment had worn off, and we had become acutely alive to the fact that we were in the soup and likely to stay there for a considerable time. Also, tobacco was beginning to run short, and our stomachs had not yet adjusted themselves to a system of rationing,

122

which, while quite good for a prison camp, was far from being what we had been accustomed to at home. We were hearty feeders who had suddenly been put on a diet, and our stomachs sat up on their hind legs and made quite a fuss about it.

Rations consisted of bread, near-coffee, jam or grease, and soup. Sometimes, instead of bread, we would get fifty small crackers apiece. When this happened, a group of men would usually club together, each contributing fifteen crackers, which would be mashed up and mixed with jam and taken to the cookhouse to be baked into a cake. It was always a problem whether it was worth sacrificing fifteen crackers to this end. The cake was always wonderful, but one's portion just slid down one's throat and was gone. Whereas one could chew a cracker.

People began to experiment with foods. One man found a bush in the corner of the yard with berries on it, and ate those – a sound move, as it turned out, for they happened by a fluke not to be poisonous. Another man used to save some of his soup at mid-day, add jam and eat the result cold in the evening. I myself got rather fond of wooden matches. You chew your match between the front teeth, then champ it up into a pulp and swallow. Shakespeare's Sonnets also make good eating, especially if you have a little cheese to go with them. And when the canteen started, we could generally get cheese.

Not much of it, of course. The way the canteen worked was that two men were allowed to go to the town with a guard and bring back as much as they could carry in a haversack apiece – the stuff being split eight hundred ways. It generally worked out at a piece of cheese about two inches long and two wide per man.

When the tobacco gave out, most of us smoked tea or straw. Tea-smokers were unpopular with the rest of their dormitory, owing to the smell caused by their activities – a sort of sweet, sickly smell which wraps itself round the atmosphere and clings for hours. Tea-smoking has also the disadvantage that it leads to a mild form of fits. It was quite usual to see men, puffing away, suddenly pitch over sideways and have to be revived with first aid.

Another drawback to Huy was that it appeared to have been expecting us even less than Liége had done. You may remember my telling you last week that our arrival seemed to come upon Liége as a complete surprise, and that there was nothing provided in the way of vessels to sip our soup out of. What Huy was short on was bedding.

An internee does not demand much in the way of bedding – give him a wisp or two of straw and he is satisfied – but at Huy it looked for a while as if there would not even be straw. However, they eventually dug us out enough to form a thin covering on the floors, but that was as far as they were able to go. Of blankets there were enough for twenty men. I was not one of the twenty. I don't know why it is, but I never am one of the twenty men who get anything. For the first three weeks, all I had over me at night was a raincoat, and one of these days I am hoping to meet Admiral Byrd and compare notes with him.

Though I probably shan't let him get a word in edgeways. He will start off on some anecdote about the winter evenings at the South Pole, and I shall clip in and say, 'Juss a minute, Byrd, jussaminute. Let me describe to you my sensations at Huy from Aug. Three, nineteen-forty, till the day my dressing-gown arrived. Don't talk to me about the South Pole – it's like someone telling Noah about a drizzle.'

Well, now you see what I meant when I said just now that what seems important to an internee merely makes the general public yawn and switch off the radio. From the rockbound coast of Maine to the Everglades of Florida, I don't suppose there is a single soul who gives a hoot that, when I was at Huy, ice formed on my upper slopes and my little pink toes dropped off one by one with frost-bite. But, boy, wait till I meet my grandchildren!

However, as somebody once observed, it is always darkest before the dawn. And, as Methusaleh said to the reporter who was interviewing him for the local sheet and had asked what it felt like to live to nine hundred – 'The first five hundred years are hard, but after that it's pie'. It was the same with us. The first seven weeks of our internment had been hard, but the pie was waiting just around the corner. There was, in short, a good time coming. On September the eighth, exactly five weeks from the day of our arrival, we were paraded and this time informed – not that Omer had received a parcel, but that we were to pack our belongings and proceed once more to an unknown destination.

This proved to be the village of Tost in Upper Silesia.

The Fifth Berlin Broadcast

I broke off last week with our eight hundred internees setting out for the village of Tost in Upper Silesia. I don't know how well acquainted my listeners are with central European geography, so I will mention that Upper Silesia is right at the end of Germany, and that Tost is right at the end of Upper Silesia – in fact, another yard or two from where we eventually fetched up, and we should have been in Poland.

We made the journey this time, not in cattle trucks but in a train divided into small compartments, eight men to the compartment, and it took us three days and three nights, during which time we did not stir from our cosy little cubbyhole. On leaving Huy, we had been given half a loaf of bread apiece and half a sausage, and after we had been thirty-two hours on the train we got another half loaf and some soup. It was at night time that the trip became rather unpleasant. One had the choice between trying to sleep sitting upright, and leaning forward with one's elbows on one's knees, in

124

which case one bumped one's head against that of the man opposite. I had never realized the full meaning of the expression 'hardheaded Yorkshireman' till my frontal bone kept colliding with that of Charlie Webb, who was born and raised in that county.

As a result of this, and not being able to wash for three days, I was not at my most dapper when we arrived at Tost Lunatic Asylum, which had been converted into a camp for our reception. But in spite of looking like something the carrion crow had brought in, I was far from being downhearted. I could see at a glance that this was going to be a great improvement on our previous resting places.

One thing that tended to raise the spirits was the discovery that Scabies had been left behind. This was the affectionate name we had given to one of our fellow-internees at Huy. He was a public menace and had given me many an uneasy moment during the five weeks in which we had been in close contact. His trouble was that he had not only got lice but had contracted a particularly contagious form of skin disease, and in his lexicon there was no such word as 'isolation'. He was a friendly, gregarious soul, who used to slink about like an alley cat, rubbing himself up against people. One time, I found him helping to peel the potatoes. Nice chap – it was a relief to find that he was no longer in our midst.

That was one thing that cheered me up on arrival at Tost. Another was that it looked as if at last we were going to have elbow-room. An Associated Press man, who came down to interview me later, wrote in his piece that Tost Lunatic Asylum was no Blandings Castle. Well, it wasn't, of course, but still it was roomy. If you had had a cat, and had wished to swing it, you could have done so quite easily in our new surroundings.

The Upper Silesian loony-bin consisted of three buildings – one an enormous edifice of red brick, capable of housing about thirteen hundred; the other two smaller, but still quite spacious. We lived and slept in the first-named, and took our meals in one of the others, where the hospital was also situated. The third building, known as the White House, stood at the bottom of the park, beyond the barbed wire, and for the first month or two was used only as a sort of clearing-station for new arrivals. Later, it was thrown open and became the center of Tost life and thought – being the place where our musicians practised and gave their concerts, where church services were held on Sundays, and where – after I had been given a padded cell to myself for working purposes – I eventually wrote a novel.

The park was a genuine park, full of trees, and somebody who measured it found that it was exactly three hundred yards in circumference. After five weeks at Huy, it looked like the Yellowstone. A high wall ran along one side of it, but on the other you got a fine view of some picturesque old barbed wire and a farm yard. There was a path running across its center which, when our sailors had provided a ball by taking a nut and winding string round it, we used in the summer as a cricket pitch.

The thing about Tost that particularly attracted me, that day of our

125

arrival, was that it was evidently a going concern. Through the barbed wire, as we paraded in front of the White House, we could see human forms strolling about, and their presence meant that we had not got to start building our little nest from the bottom up, as had been the case at Liége and Huy. For the first time, we were in a real camp, and not a makeshift.

This was brought home to us still more clearly by the fact that the reception committee included several English-speaking interpreters. And when, after we had had our baggage examined and had been given a bath, a gentleman presented himself who said that he was the Camp Adjutant, we knew that this was the real thing.

It may be of interest to my listeners to hear how a genuine civil internment camp is run. You start off with a Kommandant, some Captains and Oberleutnants and a couple of hundred soldiers, and you put them in barracks outside the barbed wire. Pay no attention to these, for they do not enter into the internee's life, and you never see anything of them except for the few who come to relieve the sentries. The really important thing is the inner camp – that is to say, the part where, instead of being outside, looking in, you are inside, looking out.

This is presided over by a Lagerführer and four Corporals, one to each floor, who are known as Company Commanders – in our case, Pluto, Rosebud, Ginger and Donald Duck. Their job is to get you up in the morning, to see that the counting of the internees on parade is completed before the Lagerführer arrives to inspect, and to pop up unexpectedly at intervals and catch you smoking in the corridor during prohibited hours.

Co-operating with these is the little group of Internee Officers – the Camp Captain, the two Camp Adjutants, the Floor Wardens and the Room Wardens. The Room Wardens ward the rooms, the Floor Wardens ward the floors, the Adjutants bustle about, trying to look busy, and the Camp Captain keeps in touch with the Lagerführer, going to see him in his office every Friday morning with hard-luck stories gleaned from the rabble, – that is to say, me and the rest of the boys. If, for instance, the coffee is cold two days in succession, the proletariat tells the Camp Captain, who tells the Lagerführer, who tells the Kommandant.

There is also another inner camp official whom I forgot to mention – the Sonderführer. I suppose the best way to describe him is to say that he is a Führer who sonders.

The great advantage of a real internment camp, like Tost, is that the internee is left to himself all through the day. I was speaking last week of the extra parades at Huy. In all my forty-two weeks at Tost, we had only three extra parades. The authorities seemed to take the view that all they wanted to know was that we were all present in the morning and also at night, so we were counted at seven-thirty a.m. and again an hour before lights-out. Except for that, we were left to ourselves.

Nor was there anything excessive in the way of discipline and formalities. We were expected to salute officers, when we met them – which we seldom

126

did, and there was a camp order that ran 'When internees are standing in groups, the first to see an officer must shout "Achtung" ', – a pleasant variant on the old game of Beaver. 'Whereat', the order continues, 'all face officer at attention, with hands on seam of trousers' – the internees' trousers, of course, – 'and look at him, assuming an erect bearing'. The only catch about this was that it gave too much scope to our humorists. A man can have a lot of quiet fun by shouting 'Achtung' and watching his friends reach for the seams of their trousers and assume an erect bearing, when there is not an officer within miles.

Life in an internment camp resembles life outside, in that it is what you make it. Nothing can take away the unpleasant feeling of being a prisoner, but you can make an effort and prevent it getting you down. And that is what we did, and what I imagine all the other British prisoners in Germany did. We at Tost were greatly helped by the fact that we had with us the sailors from the Orama, who would have cheered anyone up, and the internees from Holland.

Many of these were language teachers and musicians, and we had a great organiser in Professor Doyle-Davidson of Breda University. This meant that we were no longer restricted for intellectual entertainment to standing about in groups or playing that old Army game known alternatively as 'House' or 'Ousey-Ousey' – where you pay ten Pfennigs for a paper with numbers on it and the banker draws numbers out of a hat, and the first man to fill up his paper scoops the pool.

Lectures and concerts were arranged, and we also had revues and a straight comedy – which would have been an even bigger success than it was, but for the fact of the ingenue getting two days in the cooler right in the middle of the run.

It was also possible for us to learn French, German, Italian, Spanish, first-aid and shorthand, and also to find out all there was to find out about French and English literature. In fact, we were not so much internees as a student body. Towards the end of my stay, we had our own paper – a bright little sheet called The Tost Times, published twice a month.

One great improvement at Tost from my viewpoint, was that men of fifty and over were not liable for fatigues – in other words, the dirty work. At Liége and Huy, there had been no age limit. We had all pitched in together, reverend elders and beardless boys alike – cleaning out latrines with one hand and peeling potatoes with the other, so to speak. At Tost, the old dodderers like myself lived the life of Riley. For us, the arduous side of life was limited to making our beds, brushing the floor under and around them, and washing our linen. When there was man's work to be done, like hauling coal or shovelling snow, we just sat and looked on, swapping reminiscences of the Victorian Age, while the younger set snapped into it.

There were certain fatigues, like acting as a server at meals and working in the cookhouse, which were warmly competed for. For these, you got double rations. But the only reward of the ordinary chore, like hauling coal, was the joy of labor. I suppose a really altruistic young man after he had put in an hour or two hauling coal, would have been all pepped up by the thought that he had been promoting the happiness of the greatest number, but I never heard one of our toilers talk along these lines. It was more usual to hear them say, speaking with a good deal of feeling, that, next time their turn came along, they were ruddy well going to sprain an ankle and report sick.

It is a curious experience being completely shut off from the outer world, as one is in an internment camp. One lives principally on potatoes and rumors. One of my friends used to keep a notebook, in which he would jot down all the rumors that spread through the corridors, and they made amusing reading after the lapse of a few weeks. To military prisoners, I believe, camp rumors are known for some reason as 'Blue Pigeons'. We used to call them bedtime stories, and most dormitories would keep a corridor hound, whose duty it was to go through the corridors before lights-out, collecting the latest hot news.

These bedtime stories never turned out to be true, but a rumor a day kept depression away, so they served their purpose. Certainly, whether owing to bedtime stories or simply to the feeling, which I myself had, that, if one was in, one was in and it was no use making heavy weather about it, the morale of the men at Tost was wonderful. I never met a more cheerful crowd, and I loved them like brothers.

With this talk, I bring to an end the story of my adventures as British Civilian Prisoner Number 796, and before concluding I should like once more to thank all the kind people in America who wrote me letters while I was in camp. Nobody who has not been in a prison camp can realize what letters, especially letters like those *I* received, mean to an internee.

P. G. Wodehouse's statement to Major E. J. P. Cussen

Hotel Bristol,
Paris.
9.9.44.

Statement by Pelham Grenville Wodehouse, an Author, of the Hotel Bristol, Paris, who says:

I have been cautioned by Major Cussen that I am not obliged to say anything but that whatever I do say will be written down and may be given in evidence.

I fully understand the meaning of this caution and I desire to make a voluntary statement.

Signed: P. G. Wodehouse

I was born at Guildford, Surrey on Oct. 15th 1881 of British born parents. I was educated at Dulwich College. In 1900 I joined the Hong Kong and Shanghai Bank in London. In 1902 I left the Bank to take up a post as assistant on the "By the Way" column of "The Globe" where I remained until 1909, when I paid my second visit to America. I had first been to America for a short time in 1903. This time I made America my home but I used to come to England on short visits. From this time on I was engaged in writing short stories and novels for American magazines. The latter appeared as serials. In 1914, while in America, I married Ethel Rowley, a widow whose maiden name was Newton. My wife was a British subject when I married her and her parents were also British. In July 1914, I was on a visit to England when I had to return to the United States to fulfil a contract. In 1917 I was rejected for military service by the United States authorities on account of defective eyesight. At about this time, in partnership with Guy Bolton and Jerome Kern, I wrote a number of musical comedies.

From 1920 to 1929 my home continued to be in America but I made frequent visits to England. In 1930 and 1931 I was in Hollywood, U.S.A. where I was engaged as a writer by the Metro-Goldwyn-Mayer Corporation.

In January 1932 my wife and I went to stay at Cannes where we remained until the spring of 1934. During this time, however, we visited England for the summer of 1933.

In June 1934 we went to live at Le Touquet where in due course we bought a villa which was called "Low Wood". There we remained until the German invasion of France in 1940, with the exception of a year's visit to Hollywood from November 1936 to November 1937.

During the whole of this time I was continuing my literary work averaging one novel and several short stories a year.

At the time of the outbreak of war in September 1939 my wife and I were alone with the staff at the villa. We continued our normal existence. I was thinking out a novel. We saw a great deal at this time of Squadron No. 85 of the R.A.F. members of which were a great deal round at our house and we would also go to dinner parties with them. At this time there was no sign of war at Le Touquet. Friends of ours in the services who were in our neighbourhood visited us from time to time sometimes staying the night. We had two cars at this time and one of these we put at the disposal of the French authorities.

Sometime about the beginning of 1940 requests were made by the authorities to owners of villas to take in French doctors as guests. We had two spare bedrooms and we took two doctors including Capitaine Cambier. They were still with us when the invasion by the Germans began and remained until they were taken away by the Germans shortly before my internment. During this period we took back the car from the French authorities and gave it to Capitaine Cambier who was "officer of ravitaillement" and had to make daily journeys about the country.

During the early stages of the German advance we did not have very much uneasiness as the general feeling was that they would be repulsed before they reached Amiens. We were also reluctant to abandon our villa and its contents at a time when the neighbourhood was unprotected, but when we heard that Amiens had been given up we realised our danger. My wife then went in our little car to Étaples to seek advice from the Commanding Officer of the British Military Hospital there. He was so reassuring that we decided not to leave that day and it was only on the following day that we set out to try to get across the Somme. My wife and I started out in our Lancia car accompanied by Miss Unger the Swiss governess of Lady Furness, our neighbour, who was driving our small car which Capitaine Cambier had left behind. Unfortunately on March 17th when the roads had been covered with snow the Lancia had had a head-on collision with the Paris-Plage 'bus and, though we were not aware of it, as we had always been using the small car, it had been very inadequately repaired. Thus it broke down near Berck, and had to be abandoned in a field where it was subsequently put into some sort of shape and brought back by a British soldier. My wife and I then returned to the villa in the small car with Miss Unger.

On returning to the villa we found our neighbour Mr. Barry [Lawry] and Miss Jacqueline Grant daughter of Mr. Arthur Grant the golf professional at Le Touquet about to set out in a Ford Red Cross Van belonging to Mr. Kemp our next door neighbour who was connected with the American Red Cross. We followed them in our small car and just opposite the Golf Club house – only a few hundred yards from where we lived the Ford van broke down. The whole party then returned to their homes. My wife and I did not wish to try and go on by ourselves and leave the others behind.

For about a week everything was calm in Le Touquet, no Germans making their appearance. One German doctor arrived to inspect the Hospital and was taken there by Capt. Cambier, but I did not see him.

At the end of about a week the empty neighbouring villas were occupied by Germans except those which displayed notices shewing they were already occupied by the normal owners.

Our first contact with the Germans was when a Sergeant and a Corporal arrived and took away the greater part of our provisions and stores. After this we were left alone except that German soldiers were constantly visiting our garden and inspecting the cars. But for quite a month the only restriction placed on my movements was that I was not allowed out after 9 p.m. We settled down to a normal life and I resumed the writing of my novel.

Towards the end of June the order was given that all British subjects must report every morning at the Kommandantur in Paris-Plage. Our names were called out and we answered them; then we were free to go away. A short time later this regulation was relaxed and women were allowed to report on Saturdays only. Apart from casual conversations with an English-speaking German Major and apart from the visits to our grounds by the soldiers we had no contact with the Germans.

On July 27th a Sunday I went down to the Kommandantur to report. We were informed that we were all to be interned. We were allowed to go home and pack. I went to my home accompanied by a soldier and packed a small hand bag and was taken back to Paris-Plage. My wife was greatly distressed.

After considerable delay at the Kommandantur we started in a char-a-banc, stopping at various places to pick up other internees. Towards 10 o'c at night we reached Lille and were then driven to the prison at Loos a suburb of Lille, where we spent a week. Conditions were bad. We were then taken to the barracks at Liége for a week. Conditions were better. We then went to the citadel of Huy in Belgium. By this time our numbers had swelled to about 800 and we found the citadel very cramped. The food was scanty.

At the end of five weeks we left for Tost in Upper Silesia the journey taking three days and three nights. On arriving at Tost it was plain that conditions were going to be better as we were housed in a very large lunatic asylum with adequate grounds and there were already in residence 200 British internees from Holland.

We arrived at Tost about Sept. 12th 1940 and until the end of October conditions were hard as we had no correspondence or parcels and the potato ration was very small.

Then quite suddenly everything began to improve. Instead of three potatoes we received eight or nine and letters and parcels came in fairly regularly.

In November 1940 I was able to get writing materials, at first pencil and paper and I was able to settle down to the writing of a new novel which subsequently appeared under the title "Money in the Bank". This was thought out and written entirely during my internment.

At the time when I was interned, I had no financial anxieties as I had large investments in British Government securities and a great deal of money in my current account in New York.

I had brought with me to Tost only seven Francs, but shortly after arrival I was able to borrow fifty marks from a fellow internee. Sometime later, my American agent, Paul Reynolds arranged to have a thousand dollars sent to my wife and myself. I cannot remember what proportion of this I received but from then on I always had plenty of money.

In the camp the only use to which money could be put was in buying paper, beer, matches and tobacco. In addition, early in 1941, I was allowed to hire a typewriter for which I paid 18 marks a month. I also made frequent loans to fellow internees. There were nearly always some who needed money to buy tobacco.

When the novel "Money in the Bank" was completed about the middle of March 1941 I addressed it to Paul Reynolds, my agent, 599 Fifth Ave, New York and gave it to Professor Doyle Davidson, head of the Camp Education Committee for forwarding after censorship. It reached its destination in due course.

The other literary work I did in Tost consisted of a few chapters of the novel entitled "Full Moon", an article for the "Saturday Evening Post" entitled "My War with Germany" dealing with the humorous side of camp life in the vein of my subsequent talks on the Radio. I also condensed a short story of mine which had appeared in the "Strand Magazine" for the "Tost Times" the internees paper. There was a paper published by the Germans called "The Camp" but I never contributed to this. The article for the "Saturday Evening Post" reached them in due course.

I was receiving cheerful letters and parcels from my wife and I was frequently writing to her.

Towards the end of 1940, I was sent for to the Lager Führer's office where I was met by Angus Thuermer, an American Journalist. I think he represented Associated Press. He had obtained permission to interview me. The interview took place in the presence of the Lager Führer, Oberleutnant Buchelt, a stout officer who was, I believe, the Gestapo representative at the camp and two officers who had accompanied Thuermer from Berlin. I had no advance notice of the fact that I was to be interviewed and I had not requested such an interview.

Thuermer asked me a few general questions about conditions and how I was re-acting to them and I told him about the book "Money in the Bank". At that time I was calling it "Money for Jam". Thuermer advised me against this as the "Middle West" would not understand it. Thuermer was shewn round the Camp. I remember him coming to our dormitory. I asked him how Mr. and Mrs. Demaree Bess, of the "Saturday Evening Post" were. Though I had never met the Bess's [sic] I knew they had written to my wife offering to give any help they could and they had also written to me. Thuermer brought me some tobacco and though I cannot quite recollect if this is so I think he brought me one hundred marks. During the visit by Thuermer no mention was made of Broadcasting in any form. This was the only visit I ever received from a Journalist while I was at Tost.

Apart from anxiety about the welfare of my wife – largely dispelled by the cheerful tone of her letters – I was definitely happy at Tost. I had congenial work to occupy me and a great variety of pleasant company. As the year 1941 progressed I was approaching the age of 60 and I understood that I would then be released from internment and allowed to live with my wife privately in Germany. When I was at Loos Prison and when we were preparing to leave for Liége all the men of 60 and over were released. The only one known to me by name was my cell-mate William Cartmell who was a piano tuner living at Étaples.

When in camp I was on friendly terms with all the internees with whom I came in contact, though my intimate friends were members of my dormitory. My particular friends were Arthur Grant and Bert Haskins. The latter was one of the gardeners employed by the War Graves Commission – I think near Dunkirk.

As to the German authorities I saw very little of them but from time to time I would come across the Sonder Führer whose duty it was to act as a sort of liaison officer. Once or twice he came into the dining room while I was writing and we chatted about my work and America where he had spent a great many years. Except for him I came into contact with no German officials save when I was sent for to the Lager Führer's office which happened, I think, three times during my stay, i.e. when I was given the typewriter which he had hired for me; the "Thuermer interview" and the occasion to which I shall be referring later when I had to "turn-in" my typewriter. Of course, like everybody else, I met officers of the camp in the grounds when I "stood to attention" as everybody else did, for this was the rule. I never spoke to the Camp Kommandant who was above the Lager Führer though I remember him coming into the dining room one afternoon when I was writing there.

I never offered my services to the German authorities and was never approached by them with a view to my helping them in any way. During my time at Tost there appeared in the German-run paper called "The Camp" a very poor parody of my "Bertie Wooster" stories dealing with "Bertie" as a military man with some such signature as "P. G. Roadhouse" though I cannot remember this exactly. I had nothing to do with this and this should be obvious to anyone who has read the parody.

The first time any question of broadcasting ever arose was in the course of a very brief conversation which I had with the Lager Führer in his office. This must have been sometime in May 1941 because he left the camp towards the end of that month and his reason for sending for me was to tell me that I had to "turn-in" the typewriter which he had hired for me. He

133

referred to my article. This was an article which had been arranged for by Thuermer. It was to deal humorously with my camp experiences and was to appear, he told me, in the American Magazine "Time". What happened in America I cannot say – possibly "Time" considered the article too light – but it appeared in the "Saturday Evening Post" and was entitled "My War with Germany". Among the subjects I dealt with in it were the repulsiveness of the internees beards, the probable effect on my table manners of the dining methods at Tost and other things of a similar kind. It was light-hearted throughout.

The Lager Führer told me how much he had enjoyed the article and then said "why don't you do some broadcasts on similar lines for your American readers?" I said "I should love to" or "There's nothing I should like better" – or some similar phrase. These remarks were quite casual and made no impression on my mind.

I then saw an old copy of the "Saturday Evening Post" on the table and I said "may I look at this?" I opened it and found that it contained the final instalment of my serial "Quick Service". I showed it to him and while we were looking at the pictures another officer came in and I had to leave.

The inference I draw from this episode is either (a) that he had been told to sound me as to my willingness to broadcast or (b) that having been informed by me that I was willing – as I have described above – he reported to Berlin.

My life at Tost continued quite normally until the evening of June 21st 1941. I was playing in a cricket match when the Sonder Führer called me away and told me to go back to the dormitory and pack a bag. I went to the dormitory and packed my small valise leaving the majority of my possessions in my large suitcase. I was then taken through the barbed wire to a sort of "out-house" where I met another internee named ——— who had received the same orders as myself. We discussed the situation. His view was that we were merely going to be taken to a branch camp which had been formed in the neighbourhood. My own view was that we were going to be released as he was 60 and I was within a few weeks of being so. I also had in mind of course the activities of Mr. and Mrs. Demaree Bess. After we had been there some little time a Corporal entered with a large jug of coffee, three loaves, twelve pieces of cheese and a large dish of the soft cheese called in Germany "Quark". As the day's ration for nine men was two loaves, this perplexed us. The next thing that happened was that an officer came in and searched our bags. I had packed what I had written of my novel "Hot Water" and I pleaded to be allowed to take this, but was not permitted to do so. I sent the manuscript to Arthur Grant by the Corporal asking him to forward it and my big suitcase as soon as I could let him know where I was. Both subsequently reached me safely.

There was then a further period of waiting and we were taken to the front gate where there was a car with two "plain-clothes" men. We were driven to Gleiwitz. It was now about eight o'clock. After a very uncomfortable all night journey by train we reached the Frederickstrasse Station at Berlin somewhere between 6 and 7 in the morning. We had breakfast at the station restaurant and then walked along the Mittel Strasse trying various hotels which were all full and we were eventually taken to the Adlon.

We found the lobby of the Adlon – although it was Sunday – very bustling and crowded. This it will be remembered was the day on which Germany declared war on Russia. We were taken to a room on the 4th Floor and locked in. The room communicated by means of a bathroom with a similar bedroom which was occupied by the "plain-clothes" men. We bathed and shaved and then rested for about two hours.

Then one of the plain clothes men came in, signed to us to follow him and we went down to the lobby where he bought a paper and began to read it. —— sat down but I wanted air and so I went and walked up and down in the courtyard and while I was there my friend Major Raven von Barnikow came out. With regard to Major von Barnikow I cannot remember where and when I first met him, but I think it was in New York in 1929. He was our great friend in Hollywood paying long visits to us when he could get away from San Francisco where he was a stockbroker. He was completely American – nothing German about him. I believe his family was Swedish. His father owned large estates in Pomerania. He and I had a long conversation. He told me he had been trying to get me exchanged for a German manufacturer of screws who was an internee in England. He told me of his cousin the Baroness von Bodenhausen to whom he was engaged to be married. This surprised me as the last time I'd seen him he had been engaged to Kay Francis, the motion picture star. He said he wanted me to go to stay at the Baroness's home "Degenershausen" in the Harz mountains about 17 miles from Magdeburg. She would be in Berlin in a day or two and would take me down there. He said Werner Plack had told him I was being released so he had come to meet me.

I remembered Plack from Hollywood. I had never known him very well but had met him occasionally at parties. Von Barnikow said that Plack was in the Foreign Office. He asked after my wife and about Camp and then said that he would go to the Bristol Hotel where he was staying and get me some clothes – for I had nothing but 2 or 3 sports shirts and the suit I was wearing. As we came into the lobby we met Werner Plack.

He asked me if I was tired after my journey and how I liked Camp. It was in the course of this conversation that I mentioned the number of letters I'd received from American readers and said that it was maddening not being able to answer them.

Von Barnikow then went off to get the clothes and Plack asked me if I would like to broadcast to America.

I said: "Yes" and he said he would have me brought to his office next day to arrange the details. He then hurried off.

Shortly after this before lunch I met Lager Führer Buchelt in the lobby. He was in civilian clothes. He congratulated me on being released and I told him I was broadcasting my experiences. He made no reference to our previous conversation. He suggested a visit that afternoon to Potsdam.

We spent the afternoon at Potsdam returning in time for dinner – the party comprising ——, Buchelt, the two plain clothes men and myself.

On the following morning June 23rd, I was taken by the plain clothes men to Plack's office in the Foreign Office where he explained the method of making wax discs. After seeing him I was introduced to Dr. Phil. Paul Schmidt, not to be confused with Dr. Paul Schmidt the Press Director.

Schmidt said he had read all my books and was very complimentary about them.

—— was taken with me to the Foreign Office but did not come with me to Plack's office. One of the plain clothes men took him somewhere else in the building.

We were both taken back to the Adlon, where if I remember rightly, we lunched in the courtyard.

It is probably this lunch to which Mr. Flannery refers in his book but his statement that I said to him I was waiting for a Mr. Black or Slack who had come to see me in Camp is erroneous, as I had already met Plack, knew him sufficiently well to be aware what his name was and never met him while I was in Camp.

In the afternoon we were taken by the "plain clothes" men to the Olympic Sports Field and after —— and I were locked up in our room.

Next day Tuesday June 24th one of the plain clothes men handed me back my Passport at about 11 o'clock and then he and his companion disappeared. —— also went away. I never saw him again to speak to though I once saw him in the Adlon. —— never told me why he had been to the Foreign Office.

It is now that my recollection of events begins to get blurred, as it was at this point that the correspondents began to flock round me. I told them that I was going to broadcast.

I can remember broadcasting with Flannery, but I cannot remember the date and I recall meeting one of Hearst's men and arranging to write an article on Camp life for the Cosmopolitan magazine. This I ultimately did – I think before I left Berlin as he was in a hurry for it and was going to cable it.

On Wednesday 25th June I think I must have written and recorded my first talk and I think that it was on this day that the Baroness von Bodenhausen arrived and I met her at lunch with Baron von Barnikow.

As regards the making of the record for the first Broadcast I wrote it on the typewriter which Mrs. Bess had by now sent me and handed it to Werner Plack at the Adlon. I was driven with Plack to the Broadcasting place where the manuscript was censored by three officials each representing a branch of the authorities and I then spoke it into the device, the actual recording taking place in an adjoining room.

Plack preceded me by putting onto the record the introduction to my talk.

I think it may have been on the next day, Thursday June 26th that I did my broadcast with Flannery.

I think Friday June 27th was the day on which I went with Baroness von Bodenhausen to the Harz Mountains. The journey took about 5 hours.

With the exception of two visits to Berlin to make four other records, I remained in the Harz Mountains until near the end of November.

Now that I have explained how the broadcasts actually came to take place I should like to deal with my motives in making them. In the first place I was feeling intensely happy in a mood that demanded expression and at the same time I was very grateful to all my American friends and very desirous of doing something to return their kindness in sending me letters and parcels.

There was also, I am afraid, a less creditable motive. I thought that people, hearing the talks, would admire me for having kept cheerful under difficult conditions but I think I can say that what chiefly led me to make the talks was gratitude.

I have thought this matter over very carefully and where the account which I have just given differs from that contained in my letter to the Foreign Office I wish the former to be accepted. At the time when I wrote to the Foreign Office I was very worried.

My attitude with regard to these broadcasts can be illustrated by a series of cables exchanged between myself and Wesley Stout, Editor of the Saturday Evening Post. I have destroyed Stout's cables but presumably they are in the "Post" files. What I give here is the gist though I can recall quite a good deal of the exact wording. This exchange took place at the end of June. The incoming ones were handed to me by Plack as they were delivered at the Foreign Office. They are as follows:

1) Stout to me: "Deeply concerned by reports in Press that you are about to broadcast on German Radio. Destroys value of article now beyond recall and may jeopardize serial." The word article evidently refers to the one arranged by Thuermer when he visited me – though I was puzzled at the time.

2) Myself to Stout: "Talks cannot possibly hurt serial. Simply comic accounts of my camp life in lightest possible vein."

3) Stout to me: Repeated his warning against broadcasting and ended "people here resent what is considered your callous attitude towards England. Like serial and want to buy it but can only do so on your giving definite undertaking to stop broadcasting.

4) Myself to Stout: To the best of my recollection – After fifth talk will not speak again in any circumstances on any subject whatsoever. Cannot understand what you mean about callousness. Mine simply flippant cheerful attitude of all British prisoners. It was a point of honour with us not to whine."

My telegrams seem to me to shew a) my definite intention to make only the five camp talks and b) the absence of any bargain to obtain release by carrying on German propaganda. For my refusal to do so at this stage, had such a bargain existed, would have involved my being sent back to internment. Had there been a bargain five comic talks would never have satisfied the German authorities.

The reference in Stout's telegram No. 3 above to "your callous attitude" was almost entirely due I think to an unfortunate misrepresentation of a remark I made to one of the correspondents in Berlin. I was quoted as having said "I find it difficult to be belligerent about this war." What I actually said was "I found it difficult to be belligerent in camp", meaning by that to express in a mildly humorous way the sense of helplessness which comes over one when one finds oneself on the wrong side of the barbed wire.

On the morning after I had recorded my fifth talk, having come to Berlin from the Harz Mountains, my wife arrived at the Adlon. This would be towards the end of July.

She horrified me by telling me the effect my talks had had in England. Until then I had no notion that this resentment had been caused for I had dismissed Stout's warnings as the fussiness of an over-cautious editor.

I realised what a hideous mistake I had made and I have been longing for an opportunity ever since of putting myself right.

Before my wife arrived Plack had handed me 250 marks in payment for the five broadcasts which I accepted not realising the implications.

From that time right up to the time when I ceased to be in enemy or enemy occupied territory when Paris was liberated I never received financial assistance in any form from the German authorities either directly or indirectly.

My wife and I have spent our time as follows: To the end of November 1941 we were at Degenershausen (Baroness von Bodenhausen.) We then returned to Berlin and remained at the Adlon until April 1942, when I returned to Degenershausen my wife remaining in Berlin. I returned to Berlin (the Adlon) in November 1942 and remained there with my wife until April though for about a month I was at the Bristol because the management would not have our dog in the hotel as the result of a new rule.

In April 1943 we went as paying guests to some friends of a Frau von Wulfing, an Englishwoman whom we had got to know. Frau von Wulfing lived at 14 Bunz-Grafenstrasse in Berlin. Bertha is her christian name, and she is a widow.

Our hosts were Count and Countess Wolkenstein of Lobris near Sauer, Upper Silesia.

The Baroness von Bodenhausen had never accepted any payment from us but at the new place we were paying guests.

There we stayed until September 9th 1943 when we came to Paris spending two nights at the Bristol Hotel in Berlin. At Paris we came to the Hotel Bristol where we are today. We came to Paris because my wife was frightened of the air raids on Berlin and we thought it would be better in Paris.

We approached Doctor Schmidt for permission to leave for Paris and this was granted. Werner Plack recommended us to the Hotel Bristol.

Since my release from the camp at Tost, apart from the broadcasts I have done no work of any kind for the German authorities.

Since I was released from Tost I have written about 80 pages which were needed to complete the novel "Joy in the Morning" which I had been writing while I was interned, almost the whole of the novel called "Full Moon" which I had begun in camp, a book of camp reminiscences, a novel entitled "Spring Fever", ten short stories and about 100 pages of a novel tentatively called "Uncle Dynamite". This amounts to between 350,000 and 400,000 words and in addition to this there was the time involved in thinking out the plots. This is designed to shew that I could not have been engaged in doing secret propaganda for the enemy.

The novels "Joy in the Morning" and "Full Moon" and two short stories were taken to America by Mr. Robert Chalker of the American Embassy in Berlin upon his return to the United States in about April 1942 – on repatriation.

As regards my finances I have handed to Major Cussen a note which I have prepared setting out the position fully. I am anxious that he should discuss it with my wife who can supply any additional details which may be desirable.

I have handed to Major Cussen a Journal which I made from time to time during my internment. I drew upon this for my book of camp reminiscences and also for the broadcasts which I made at Berlin.

I should like to conclude by saying that I never had any intention of assisting the enemy and that I have suffered a great deal of mental pain as the result of my action.

I have read this statement and it is true. It was commenced at the Hotel Bristol, Paris on Sept. 9th 1944, continued on Sept. 10th and 11th and concluded today Sept. 12th.

Signed: P. G. Wodehouse.

Statement written down and signature witnessed by:

E. J. P. Cussen
Major. I.C.
12.9.44.

Appendix Three
Financial statement by P. G. Wodehouse

P. G. Wodehouse and Mrs. Wodehouse – Financial Statement.

Money received in Berlin:

1. From sale of bracelet	40,000 marks
2. Borrowed from Frau Schwarbach	10,000 marks
3. Borrowed from von Barnikow	5,000 marks
4. Sale of wrist-watch to Frau Herbsch	5,000 marks
5. Received from Jepsen in exchange for cheques on our American account	8,000 marks
6. Cash in possession at time of my release, from Paul Reynolds, my agent in New York	1,000 marks

Total 69,000 marks

Note: I also received some money for royalties on my books from Messrs Tauchnitz, but have forgotten how much – I think about 1,000 marks.

Money spent in Berlin: Roughly 25,000 marks. We took 30,000 marks to Paris, thus leaving in Berlin about 25,000 [sic] marks.

In Paris. Money received:

1. From Count Sollohub	140,000 francs
2. From Jose Janes of Barcelona, my Spanish publisher	320,000 francs
3. From Rotje, picture dealer	25,000 francs

Total 485,000 francs

Appendix Four
Ethel Wodehouse's statement to Major E. J. P. Cussen

Hotel Bristol
Paris.
Sep. 12 1944.

Statement by Ethel Wodehouse, wife of Pelham Grenville Wodehouse, who says:

After my husband was interned by the Germans on July 27th, 1940, my movements were as follows:

(1) At le Touquet for 3 or 4 days.
(2) At Saint Georges with Mme Bernard after our villa had been taken over by the Germans.
(3) About the end of October, 1940, I obtained a permit to go to Lille, where I stayed in a furnished bed-sitting room until the Spring of 1941.
(4) About April, 1941, I went to stay with Mme Derocquigny at Veil Hesdin at Chateau le Fontal.

From time to time I received cheerful letters and postcards from my husband which I have handed to Major Cussen.

It was while I was at Chateau le Fontal that I heard rather a garbled account to the effect that my husband had broadcast from Germany and that he had been called a traitor in the English newspapers.

I think it was at the end of July that I joined my husband in Berlin at the Adlon Hotel. As soon as I saw my husband I told him what I had heard about the resentment in England caused by his broadcasting. He did not at first appreciate how or why this resentment had come about.

My journey to Berlin from Veil Hesdin was arranged by the German authorities. An Army Officer called on me and told me that he had good news – my husband had been released. I was to go to Berlin when I was ready. The same officer later escorted me to Busselles [sic] and thence I was escorted to the Adlon Hotel, Berlin, by a civilian, a man.

Throughout the whole of my time in Germany and France I have never done anything to help the enemy.

I have examined the Financial Statement prepared by my husband. I am, I think, more familiar than he is with the details of our money arrangements. I make the following observations:

(1) The bracelet was sold to Herr Knack, Jeweller, Oliver Platz No. 10, Berlin (Tel: 925006).
(2) Frau Schwarbach was a widow who had been married to a Jew (first name Charlotte). Her address in Berlin is: Salchsische Str. No. 6.

141

I agreed to pay, in London, when I could, in English money the sum of 10,000 marks to:

her daughter – Mrs. Greta Gruenfeld
and her son – Erik Schwarbach.

This transaction was arranged at Frau von Wulfing's on April 8th, 1943 (14 Borggraffen Str., Berlin).

(3) No comments.
(4) Frau Herbst, I think, lived at the Kaisarhof [sic] Hotel and was a casual acquaintance.

Signed: Ethel Wodehouse

Appendix Five

Letter from P. G. Wodehouse to Major E. J. P. Cussen

Hotel Bristol
Rue Faubourg St Honoré
Paris
Sept 14. 1944

Dear Major Cusson [sic].

I should like this letter to be appended to my statement, as it contains information which H.M. Government will wish to have regarding my case.

When I was in Germany, I had several offers to write, as my books have always been very popular in that country. All these I refused, as I recognised the impossibility of doing any writing of any description (other than novels for post-war publication) during the war. Among them was one from the Ufa Film Co, who wanted me to do a humorous film for Jenny Jugo, the comedienne. And Edward Kunneke, the composer, whose work is well known in England, was anxious that I should write a comic opera with him. Both these offers I refused.

Early in 1942 I was approached by Fraulein Charlotte Serda with an offer from the Berliner Film Co, who wished to make a picture of one of my novels, to be selected by them. I did not mention this to you on Sept 12, as my copy of the contract has been lost and I thought it might be better to wait until the British authorities were in a position to verify my statements by reference to the files of the Berliner Film Co. But on reflection I felt that this would be wrong, so I supply the details herewith.

The novel they selected was my *Heavy Weather*. This is a comedy story dealing with the adventures at Blandings Castle of Sue Brown, the chorus girl, and her fiancé, Ronnie Fish, nephew of the Earl of Emsworth, and centres round the duel between Lady Julia Fish, Ronnie's mother, who is trying to break the match, and Sue's ally, the Hon. Galahad Threepwood, Lord Emsworth's brother, a genial old gentleman who long ago had been in love with Sue's mother. Lord Emsworth's prize pig, Empress of Blandings, plays an important part, as do Beach, his butler, and Pilbeam, a private detective whom Lord Emsworth has engaged to protect his pig against an anticipated attack on it by a neighbour who owns the pig which is its rival for the Fat Pigs silver medal at the Shropshire Agricultural Show. The whole book is in the lightest possible vein.

Such a story could not possibly be twisted for propaganda purposes, but nevertheless I insisted on the insertion in the contract of a clause whereby I was given assurance that nothing of this kind would be attempted. I was also given to understand that the picture would not be released until after the war, Fraulein Serda telling me that there was a considerable list of pictures scheduled which had to precede it. And when they assured me that the scene of the story would be changed from Shropshire to Pomerania and that all the characters would be German, I had no further uneasiness and closed with the offer. In due course I received payment of 40,000 marks, 10 per cent of which I paid to Fraulein Serda as agent's commission. (I cannot remember Fraulein Serda's address, as our meetings took place at the Adlon Hotel, but she can be easily traced, as her father is a well-known figure on the Berlin Stage.)

In the light of my conversation with you on September 12, I now see for the first time that the sale of this book may be considered to come under the head of trading with the enemy, and if H.M. Government decides that this is so, I must of course accept the penalty. But I am hoping that they will take a lenient view, realising that I acted in perfect innocence, on the assumption that only commercial undertakings came within the scope of the law relating to trading with the enemy, and that there would be no objection to a transaction of a purely artistic nature. It was for this reason, and acting on this assumption, that I later sold my novel *Money in the Bank* to Messrs. Tauchnitz. Apart from these two transactions, I had no dealings with any firm of any kind during my stay in Germany.

I need scarcely say how deeply I regret my folly.

Yours sincerely

P. G. Wodehouse.

Appendix Six

Further financial statement by P. G. Wodehouse

Hotel Bristol
Paris.
15.9.44

Further Statement by Pelham Grenville Wodehouse who says:
I have been cautioned by Major Cussen that I am not obliged to say anything but that whatever I do say will be written down and may be given in evidence.

I fully understand the meaning of this caution and I desire to make a voluntary statement additional to that which I have already made.

Signed: P. G. Wodehouse.

Since I prepared my Financial Statement I have addressed a letter to Major Cussen dated Sept. 14 1944. In this letter I describe how I received, while in Germany, a sum of 40,000 marks from the Berliner Film Co.

I have also discussed our financial position with my wife. As a result I wish to say that while the account of income given in my financial statement is correct to the best of my belief the account of expenditure is too small. I fear that it is impossible for me at this time to deal adequately with expenditure but I will do my best later on.

I have read this statement and it is true.

Signed: P. G. Wodehouse.

Witness: E. J. P. Cussen.
Major. I.C.
15.9.44.

Further financial statement by Ethel Wodehouse

Hotel Bristol, Paris.
Sep. 15 1944.

Further Statement by Ethel Wodehouse, wife of Pelham Grenville Wodehouse, who says:

While my husband and I were in Germany he had a banking account at the Commerz Bank – about ten minutes walk from the Adlon Hotel. I had authority to draw on that account.

In London we each have an account at the National Provincial Bank, 57 Aldwych.

My husband also has a small account at the Hong Kong and Shanghai Bank – for sentimental reasons.

In New York we each have an account at the National City Bank, 42nd Street.

When we left Berlin I left behind with Werner Plack a sum of money in German marks. I cannot remember exactly how much this was but it was a large sum.

I left this sum of money with him because he said that I would not be able to get permission to take it with me to France. He had arranged for me to take a large sum of money to France, but I had more than was covered by his arrangement.

Plack promised that he would get the remaining sum to me in Paris within two months. Whenever I saw him in Paris I used to remind him but he always promised to deal with the matter, but never did so.

Shortly before Plack left Paris prior to the liberation he promised faithfully that I should have the money.

Thus a few days before Major Cussen reached Paris, I called at the Swiss Consulate to see if they had any money from Plack for me. I thought it might come through the Swiss as they were protecting British interests.

I saw a Mr. Amsler though I cannot be sure of the name, and I told him what I had come about. He said he would ring me up later.

Later I saw him again at the Consulate and he said he had some money for me. He gave 560,000 francs and I gave him a receipt.

I do not know exactly how this money is made up but it is no doubt made up of the money I handed to Plack and of the balance left in my husband's account at the Commerz Bank in Berlin, but I think Plack still has some of my money.

I have read this statement and it is true.

Signed: Ethel Wodehouse.

Appendix Eight

Report by Major Cussen on behalf of M.I.5 and the Home Office

I

Introduction

1.   In June, July and August 1941, the well known author P. G.Wodehouse made certain broadcasts from Berlin. He had been in France and, falling into the hands of the Germans in May 1940, he had in due course been interned. As a well known public figure he had been the subject of reports in the British and American Press, but he had hitherto been regarded merely as one of the unfortunate people who had been unable to leave France before it was over-run by the enemy.

It came as a considerable shock to the public to hear his voice on the German radio and to learn that he was apparently not in internment but living at the Hotel Adlon, Berlin. As will be hereafter described, he became the subject of severe condemnation by the Press and by the public and his name was associated with that of William Joyce ("Lord Haw Haw") and other traitors.

2.   So far as the authorities were concerned, little reliable information as to the circumstances in which Wodehouse broadcast was available in 1941 and little additional information became available thereafter during the course of the war. The authorities did, however, regard the case of Wodehouse as one which must be the subject of enquiry at the proper time upon the basis that he was a British subject who had given assistance to the enemy. On May 6th, 1944 his name was included in the list of British subjects in enemy occupied territory whose cases required investigation, this list being sent to Supreme Headquarters, Allied Expeditionary Force.

3.   On the evening of Tuesday, August 29th, 1944, the Security Service were informed that a message had been received in London from the Officer Commanding one of the Special Counter-Intelligence Units in Paris, stating that Wodehouse was at the Hotel Bristol, Paris, and asking for instructions.

On Wednesday, August 30th, the Security Service informed the Home Office that Wodehouse was in Paris. On August 31st the Home Office informed the Security Service that they did not wish Wodehouse to be brought to the United Kingdom but that they requested the Security Service to send an officer to Paris to make such enquiries on the spot as might be appropriate.

4.   I was instructed to go to Paris for this purpose and I arrived there on the evening of September 5th. In due course I interviewed Wodehouse, his wife and certain other persons, a statement being taken, under caution, from Wodehouse. Certain other statements were taken by me from persons who were able to give information as to the conduct of Wodehouse and his wife while in Paris.

The purpose of this report is to indicate the result of these enquiries. A stage has, however, been reached where it is convenient to review the case and to set out the whole of the information at present available. In the course of this report an endeavour will be made to accomplish this task.

II

The career of Wodehouse up to September 3rd, 1939

5.   Wodehouse was born at Guildford, Surrey on October 15th, 1881, his parents being British. He was educated at Dulwich College and in 1900 entered the service of the Hong Kong and Shanghai Bank in London. In 1902 he left the Bank and until 1909 was a member of the staff of "The Globe". In that year he made his home in America, a country which he had already visited, and it appears that, apart from visits to England, he there remained until 1932.

Wodehouse states that from 1909 onwards he was engaged in writing short stories and novels, a number of the latter appearing in American magazines as serials. In 1914, while in America, he married Ethel Rowley, a widow, who is a British subject.

6.   Wodehouse did not serve in the 1914–18 war. In July 1914 he was in England but returned in that month to the United States to fulfil a contract. In 1917 he was rejected for military service by the United States authorities on account of defective eyesight.

7.   By this time Wodehouse, in partnership with Guy Bolton and Jerome Kern, was writing a number of musical comedies and his career as a successful author appears to have become well established. In 1930 and 1931 he was under contract to the Metro-Goldwyn-Mayer Corporation at Hollywood. In 1932 Wodehouse and his wife visited Cannes, remaining until 1934 during which time they visited England in the summer of 1933.

In June 1934 the Wodehouse bought a villa at Le Touquet called "Low Wood" and, apart from one year which they spent in Hollywood, they now made their home at Le Touquet.

8.   Wodehouse by now was a rich man and from general enquiries which I have made there is no doubt that he lived a very comfortable life at Le

Touquet. He was intensely interested in his literary work and preferred to a great extent to leave social activities to his wife. She devoted herself to these with considerable zest. In June 1939 Wodehouse received the Honorary Degree of Doctor of Letters from the University of Oxford.

There is no doubt that Wodehouse, as the creator of such characters as "Bertie Wooster" and "Jeeves", had acquired a widespread reputation in this country, excelled perhaps only in the United States. I understand that his books had obtained a large sale on the Continent and that they had been translated into many of the European languages.

9. There is one incident which Wodehouse described to me in conversation and which was at the time reported in the Press, which it may be appropriate to mention here. While under contract in Hollywood to the Metro-Goldwyn-Mayer Corporation in 1931 he received, for a year's work, something in the neighbourhood of £20,000. One day he was being interviewed by the Press and he told them that he did very little work in return for this large sum of money, and that most of his time was spent waiting to be told what was expected of him. This was widely reported in the American Press and attracted the attention of financial interests who were supporting the film industry, including the Corporation by whom Wodehouse was employed. They made use of Wodehouse's remarks to probe the conduct of his employers from the financial point of view with the result that the latter vented their rage on Wodehouse, and it was not until 1936 that friendly relations were restored between Wodehouse and Hollywood.

I mention this incident because it does serve to show that Wodehouse is in some degree at all events lacking in worldly wisdom, for it is to his lack of this quality, which he recognises, that he attributes his conduct in Germany during the present war.

III

Wodehouse's life from the outbreak of war
until his internment by the Germans in July 1940

10. The outbreak of war found the Wodehouses at their villa in Le Touquet. Wodehouse states that they continued their normal existence. He mentions, in his statement, that members of No. 85 Squadron of the Royal Air Force frequently visited his home, as did Service friends generally who were in the neighbourhood. Capitaine Cambier and another doctor of the French Army Medical Service were taken as guests in the villa, and one of Wodehouse's motor cars was lent first to the French local authorities and later to Capitaine Cambier.

11. Wodehouse describes in his statement his feelings at the time of the

German advance through France in May 1940. It was not, he says, until the enemy had occupied Amiens that he and his wife realised their danger. His wife sought the advice of the Commanding Officer of the British Military Hospital at Étaples who appears to have reassured her, but finally the Wodehouse's made their first effort to escape the Germans. This was ineffective in its first phase on account of the breakdown of their car and in its second phase, when they set off in another car, on account of the breakdown of a Ford van in which were travelling a Mr. Barry [sic for Lawry] and a Miss Jacqueline Grant. Wodehouse says that his wife and he did not wish to try and go on by themselves and leave the occupants of the Ford van behind, and the whole party therefore returned to their homes in Le Touquet and awaited events.

He then describes his first contact with the enemy; certain provisions and stores were removed from his villa; German soldiers visited his grounds; he was not allowed to be out after 9 p.m.

12.   Towards the end of June all British subjects had to report daily at the Kommandantur in Paris-Plage. He says that he settled down to a normal life and went on with the writing of the novel upon which he was engaged.

On Sunday, July 27th, upon reporting at the Kommandantur he and other male British subjects were informed that they were to be interned. He went home in order to pack and parted with his wife.

I have little doubt that, although Wodehouse may sometimes find the energy of his wife in social activities a source of difficulty, he is genuinely attached to her and moreover relies upon her considerably to arrange the ordinary affairs of life for him.

It is, I think, right to point out that for the first time in many years Wodehouse, who had always been able to rely upon the advice of his wife, his literary agents, his accountants and the like, was now placed in a position where he had to make decisions for himself.

13.   Before leaving this stage of the events which are being described it may be said that opportunity will be taken to check the account given by Wodehouse by interviewing Mr. Arthur Grant of Le Touquet, who has recently arrived in this country, his daughter Miss Jacqueline Grant who is with him, and Capitaine Cambier who is believed to be residing at present in Paris at 7 Avenue Alphonse XIII. It may also be possible to obtain information about the conduct of the Wodehouses at the time of the Germans advance from some of their friends who were in the Services and who, according to Wodehouse, visited them as has already been described, and from other residents at Le Touquet.

I say this because among the matters which have featured in the attacks upon Wodehouse in the Press and elsewhere is a story to the effect that he was giving a cocktail party at the time when the Germans arrived, with the inference that he made no effort to reach the United Kingdom but rather the reverse.

Although it is not possible to say what we shall ascertain from the further enquiries envisaged, I do not think we shall find that the "cocktail party" story is a correct one.

14.   I shall not be surprised if some of those we shall interview criticise the attitude which the Wodehouses, and Mrs Wodehouse in particular, adopted towards the Germans. I doubt very much whether either Wodehouse or his wife, even at this early stage, had any idea of the proper standard of conduct on such occasions. If the Germans adopted a tolerant attitude towards them, both the Wodehouses would, in my view, be inclined to respond too readily, Wodehouse in particular being very susceptible to any form of flattery.

IV

Wodehouse's life in internment

15.   Wodehouse was taken first to Lille, thence to Liége and later to Huy in Belgium, and finally after some five weeks to Tost in Upper Silesia where with other internees he was lodged in premises which had formerly been used as a lunatic asylum. He states that he arrived at Tost about September 12th, 1940. Wodehouse gives an account of the conditions prevailing at Tost, and this may be summarised by saying that before long, under arrangements made by his American agent, he received a certain amount of money; that he was allowed to continue his literary work and that he completed a novel called "Money in the Bank". He also wrote an article for the "Saturday Evening Post" on the humorous side of camp life called "My War with Germany", and condensed a short story which had appeared in the Strand Magazine for the "Tost Times", a paper run by the internees themselves.

16.   Before dealing with the account which Wodehouse gives in his statement of certain events which occurred during his time at Tost, such as the arrival of an American journalist called Angus Thuermer, of Associated Press, to interview him, it is desirable to mention certain allegations which have been made by persons repatriated from Tost. These are of a somewhat vague character but, in view of the rather unusual circumstances of this investigation involving as it did the interviewing of a man who might be uncertain of what was alleged against him, I thought it right to bring them to the notice of Wodehouse at the time when I saw him. I pointed out to him that I was not suggesting that they were necessarily well founded, but that I was merely informing him of them in case he wished to deal with them. Certain of the matters dealt with in his statement are there found as a result.

151

17. The allegations which I put to him were as follows:
    (i) A merchant seaman (Gibson) reported that it was "rumoured in the camp" that Wodehouse had put in an application to go to America in order to write propaganda for the Germans.
    (ii) An Australian seaman (Urban Jones) said that he had "heard" at Tost that Wodehouse had written to the German Foreign Office offering his services.
    (iii) A former internee (Harvey) reported that Wodehouse "was notorious" among the internees as having been pro-German.
    (iv) A former internee (Dr. Steel) reported that "there was no doubt that Wodehouse collaborated with the Germans". An American journalist had visited Tost and had persuaded him to write "a very glowing account" of life in camp. Wodehouse had submitted to the internees' "Contact Committee" a letter to the German authorities in which he offered to write articles for them to promote better feeling between the French and the Germans. This Committee of internees refused to pass this letter on.
    (v) It was alleged by a repatriated merchant seaman that a weekly paper called "The Camp" (a German publication for circulation in internment camps) was edited by Wodehouse and was pro-German in tone.

It is quite probable, of course, that similar allegations may be made against Wodehouse as more former internees from Tost reach this country and these will all be the subject of examination.

18. Wodehouse deals with these allegations in the following way:
    (i) "As to the German authorities, I saw very little of them . . ." He then describes the circumstances in which he would normally meet officials, etc.
    (ii) "I never offered my services to the German authorities and was never approached by them with a view to my helping them in any way. During my time at Tost there appeared in the German-run paper called 'The Camp' a very poor parody of my 'Bertie Wooster' stories dealing with 'Bertie' as a military man, with some such signature as 'P. G. Roadhouse' though I cannot remember this exactly. I had nothing to do with this and this should be obvious to anyone who has read the parody."
    (iii) Wodehouse relates how, towards the end of 1940, he was summoned to the Lager Führer's office where he found Angus Thuermer of Associated Press. Wodehouse did not ask for such an interview and he states that he had no prior information of its imminence. According to Wodehouse, apart from questions as to camp conditions which Thuermer asked the main subject of discussion was the novel on which Wodehouse was engaged and

which was then entitled "Money for Jam". Thuermer advised Wodehouse that his title would not be understood by some American readers, and indeed Wodehouse ultimately changed the title to "Money in the Bank". Wodehouse was in possession of a cutting from an American newspaper called, I believe, "News Journal" which published, no doubt in common with many other American newspapers, a cable from Thuermer describing this interview. A copy of this will be found in the bundle of documents circulated with this report and this is in conformity with the account of the interview given by Wodehouse. Wodehouse maintains that broadcasting was not mentioned at all during this interview.

V

Wodehouse's frame of mind while in internment at Tost

19.   In his statement Wodehouse says that, once his anxiety about his wife was dispelled by the cheerful tone of her letters, he was definitely happy at Tost. He was able to continue his writing; he claims that he was on friendly terms with all the internees with whom he came in contact, in particular with Mr. Arthur Grant and with Mr. Bert Haskins. As has been already remarked, he had received some money and he says that this was sufficient for all his camp needs. As to his general financial position he, unlike many internees, had no anxiety. Although it is not mentioned in his statement, he told me that to the best of his knowledge his assets at this time were as follows:

British Government securities held by Wodehouse £56,763
British Government securities held by Mrs. Wodehouse ..   £48,523
At the National City Bank, New York $100,000
(approx)

He was going to reach the age of sixty on October 15th, 1941, and he understood that he would then be released from internment and that he would be able to live privately with his wife in Germany. I understand that this was the practice of the German authorities, but this has yet to be officially verified.

20.   Mrs. Wodehouse produced to me a number of letters and postcards addressed to her by her husband from Tost. These are cheeful in tone and it is not without interest that they appear to indicate that, up to June 14th 1941, Wodehouse had no idea that his release was imminent for, in a letter bearing that date, he mentions that he has sufficient tobacco for the present.
    Wodehouse handed to me the manuscript, written in pencil, of a journal which he kept while at Tost. This was not kept day-by-day but entries were

153

made at such times as something struck him as being interesting. I think it may fairly be said that the conclusion to be drawn from the terms of the entries in this journal is that Wodehouse was as content with his lot as any internee is likely to be and that he was utilising to the full the opportunities which he had of observing the conduct of a number of different types at close quarters, and was enjoying the process.

21.   The journal has been examined with a view to seeing whether Wodehouse expresses therein any sympathy with the enemy. The following entries are those which are relevant:

(i) July 31st, 1940. –
    ". . . I was first to alight from train. Met old German general asked how old I was, felt my suitcase and said it was too heavy to carry and sent for truck – asked me if I had had anything to eat or drink. Very sympathetic and kindly . . ."

(ii) August 15th, –
    ". . . The reason for forbidding letters is apparently that there has been a lot of sabotage at Lille, people cutting telephone wires etc., so I am told by very nice, sympathetic German lieutenant . . ."

(iii) September 8th, –
    ". . . The journey to Tost . . . our dear old Sergeant is with us, and the sight of him does much to take away that lost feeling. He is more like a mother than a sergeant . . ."

(iv) October 8th, –
    ". . . got into conversation with charming German corporal who spoke perfect English and has read all my books. Also another one had, which bucked me up enormously . . ."

(v) October 30th, –
    ". . . I am very fond of the two interpreters I have talked with, one grey haired (43), fresh face, veteran of last war, the other the spectacled one, who learned his English in U.S.A. (He worked for Fred Harvey hotels as newstand, and says 'Have you got me, boys?') It bears out what I have always said that Germans are swell guys, and the only barrier between us is the one of language. I have never met an English-speaking German whom I didn't like instantly . . ."

Having regard to the circumstances in which this journal was written, I do not think any very great exception can fairly be taken even to these entries. The latter part of the entry quoted in sub-paragraph (v) above may contain sentiments with which one definitely disagrees, but Wodehouse is not the first person to have expressed such views. It must be a matter of opinion as to whether the entry in question affords an indication of the existence of a state of mind which would tend towards co-operation with the enemy.

The original letters and the original journal are in my possession and are available for examination. It has not been thought necessary at the present stage to have these copied.

22.   One of the matters which has greatly troubled the public in this country is the suggestion that Wodehouse made a bargain with the Germans and that he agreed to broadcast in order to obtain his release. The documents which I have just dealt with may be of value in assessing the position in this regard for, if Wodehouse was reasonably content and free from anxiety, as seems to have been the case, it may be reasonable to assume that he would be less likely to enter into a bargain than if the reverse were true. Moreover, Wodehouse claims that he was confident that he would be released in October 1941, on attaining the age of sixty. If, of course, factual evidence is later obtained as to acts of collaboration with the enemy by Wodehouse while at Tost, the position will be altered.

When Mr. Arthur Grant is interviewed attention will be paid to any information which he can give as to Wodehouse's life at Tost and a similar course will be adopted when other interviews with former internees are possible.

VI

The first mention of the possibility of Wodehouse broadcasting

23.   In May 1941, says Wodehouse, he was sent for by Oberleutnant Buchelt, the Lager Führer at Tost. Buchelt was about to leave Tost and he told Wodehouse that he must hand back the typewriter which he, Buchelt, had obtained for him and for which Wodehouse paid a monthly rental of 18 marks. Buchelt referred to Wodehouse's light article "My War with Germany" which had appeared in the "Saturday Evening Post". According to Wodehouse, Oberleutnant Buchelt said that he had enjoyed the article and added, "Why don't you do some broadcasting on similar lines for your American readers?" Wodehouse replied, "I should love to" "There is nothing I should like better", or in some similar phrase.

"These remarks were quite casual and made no impression on my mind" is the way in which Wodehouse deals with this incident in his statement.

24.   We shall only be able to check Wodehouse's account of this incident and to judge whether it really was the origin of the broadcasting question when we are able to interview Oberleutnant Buchelt, if he is still alive, and to examine all the documents relating to the Wodehouse case which may be in the records of the various German Government Departments concerned.

VII

Wodehouse is removed from Tost to Berlin – June 21st, 1941
The broadcasts are arranged and take place

25. On the evening of June 21st, continues Wodehouse, he was interrupted while playing in a cricket match at Tost and ordered to pack a bag. He was taken through the barbed wire to a hut where he found a fellow internee named —— who had received similar instructions. Certain rations were issued to them, their bags were searched and they were then taken by motor car to Gleiwitz. There they boarded a train for Berlin and, after travelling through the night, reached the Friedrichstrasse Station in that city between six and seven in the morning. Their escort consisted of two "plain clothes" men. The escort with their prisoners went to several hotels near the railway station but were unable to find accommodation, and the party eventually reached the Adlon Hotel where rooms were obtained on the fourth floor. Wodehouse and —— were in a bedroom, the door of which was locked; a bathroom led through to another bedroom which was occupied by the escort. After resting, the two prisoners were taken to the ground floor of the hotel and, while they were there, Wodehouse walked in the courtyard.

26. There he was joined by a friend, one Major Raven von Barnikow, whom he had known since 1929 and with whom he had been on friendly terms in Hollywood. Von Barnikow told him that he had been endeavouring to secure his release and that he had learned from one Werner Plack that the release was to take place, hence his, von Barnikow's arrival at the Adlon Hotel. He suggested that Wodehouse should go and stay at the house of his cousin, the Baroness von Bodenhausen, near Magdeburg.
   Before long Werner Plack himself joined Wodehouse and von Barnikow. Wodehouse remembered that Plack was a German who had been in Hollywood and whom he had occasionally met. According to von Barnikow, Plack was now attached to the German Foreign Office.
   According to Wodehouse, Plack enquired as to his journey, and in conversation Wodehouse mentioned the number of letters which he had received from his American readers and said "it was maddening not being able to answer them".

27. Wodehouse continues "von Barnikow then went off to get the clothes (for Wodehouse) and Plack asked me if I would like to broadcast to America. I said 'yes' and he said he would have me brought to his office the next day to arrange the details. He then hurried off. Shortly after this, before lunch, I met Lager Führer Buchelt in the lobby. He was in civilian clothes. He congratulated me on being released and I told him I was broadcasting my experiences. He made no reference to our previous con-

156

versation . . ." Buchelt,——and Wodehouse, and the escort, spent the afternoon sightseeing.

28. Wodehouse describes how on the following morning, June 23rd, both he and —— were taken to the Foreign Office by their escort. Wodehouse does not know what happened to —— but he himself was interviewed by Plack and the method of making wax discs for broadcasting purposes was explained. Wodehouse also saw Dr Paul Schmidt of the Foreign Office. Wodehouse told me that Dr Schmidt was the official who used to act as interpreter for Hitler at conferences. In due course —— and Wodehouse were taken back to the Adlon Hotel where they had lunch, and in the afternoon did some more sight-seeing with their escort.

On the next day, Tuesday June 24th, one of the "plain clothes" men handed Wodehouse his passport in the morning and then withdrew with his colleague. Wodehouse says that —— also went away. According to Wodehouse, —— never told him why he, ——, had been taken to the Foreign Office, nor did they ever speak to each other again.

29. "It is now," says Wodehouse, "that my recollection of events begins to get blurred as it was at this point that the correspondents began to flock around me. I told them I was going to broadcast."

It is difficult, having regard to the inability of Wodehouse to recollect with any clarity the events which now followed, to present any clear picture of them. Indeed, as to one event of the previous day, i.e. a conversation with the American radio reporter Harry Flannery, Wodehouse is also vague in the extreme.

30. It is sufficient, perhaps, to say here that Wodehouse was interviewed by a number of journalists and that, having by now typed out his first broadcast script on a typewriter which was brought to him at the Adlon Hotel, he went with Plack to a studio of some kind and there recorded Talk No. 1 in his series, Plack first recording an introduction. By now, the radio reporter Harry Flannery, who was employed by the American Columbia Broadcasting System, had arranged a radio interview with Wodehouse to take place before a microphone in Berlin, whence it would be transmitted to the United States. Wodehouse was under the impression that this radio interview actually took place on Thursday, June 26th, but according to information furnished to the Security Service by the British Broadcasting Corporation, this actually took place on June 27th. According to Wodehouse, on that date, which was a Friday, he left Berlin with Baroness von Bodenhausen and reached her home in the Hartz Mountains. He adds that, with the exception of two visits to Berlin to make the four records required to complete his series of five talks, he remained at the home of this lady until the end of November 1941.

At this stage of the enquiry we are dependent, for the information as to the events mentioned above, on Wodehouse alone, though Flannery has described his part in them in a book, as will later be mentioned.

VIII

Comments on the account given by Wodehouse of his arrival in Berlin, and the arranging of his broadcasts

31. Wodehouse maintains that at the time when he was suddenly removed from the Camp at Tost, he had no idea that it was going to be suggested to him in Berlin that he should broadcast. It is, of course, very significant that one of the people who were in the Adlon Hotel on the day when Wodehouse arrived there was Oberleutnant Buchelt, the former Lager Führer at Tost. Only when we are able, should this be possible, to interview Buchelt, Werner Plack and Dr Schmidt and to examine the German official records shall we be able to confirm or disprove the account which Wodehouse gives of the arrangements for his broadcasts.

32. It is also significant that —— was brought to Berlin with Wodehouse. —— is believed by the Security Service to have collaborated with the enemy and his name is on the list which has been sent to S.H.A.E.F. We hope to be able to interview —— in due course and to hear his account of his arrival with Wodehouse in Berlin.

33. I am bound to say that I have some misgivings as to the account given by Wodehouse of this all-important stage in his activities, but he gave it after considerable reflection and he claims that it is correct.

IX

Harry W. Flannery, the American radio reporter

34. In his book "Assignment to Berlin", published in London by Michael Joseph Ltd in 1942, at page 244 onwards, Flannery gives an account of his meeting with Wodehouse at the Adlon Hotel in Berlin and of the arrangements which were made for the interview between himself and Wodehouse before a microphone, which was broadcast to the United States. It is unnecessary to set out in full the material contained therein, which is not altogether favourable to Wodehouse. Flannery leaves one in no doubt that he thought Wodehouse was a most stupid person and without any political sense. It is proposed to interview Flannery when possible.

35.   Flannery, at page 249, gives his impressions of the background of the matter as follows: "By this time the Wodehouse plot was evident. It was one of the best Nazi publicity stunts of the war, the first with a human angle. That was because it was not the work of Dr. Goebbels but of Hollywood-wise Plack instead. Plack had gone to the camp near Gleiwitz to see Wodehouse and found that the author was completely without political sense, and had an idea. He suggested to Wodehouse that, in return for being released from the prison camp, he write a series of broadcasts about his experiences; there would be no censorship and he would put them on the air himself. In making that proposal Plack showed that he knew his man. He knew that Wodehouse made fun of the English in his stories and that he seldom wrote in any other way, that he was still living in the period about which he wrote and had no conception of Nazism and all that it meant. Wodehouse was his own Bertie Wooster".

36.   According to Wodehouse, Plack had never visited him at the camp and the broadcasts were not made as a condition of release. It may be that Oberleutnant Buchelt conveyed his idea as to broadcasts by Wodehouse to Plack who was quick to take advantage of it. On the other hand Plack may have instructed Buchelt to sound Wodehouse. These matters can only be cleared up when enquiries in Berlin become possible.

When I interviewed Wodehouse I thought it right to read to him certain extracts from Flannery's book but, as has been mentioned, Wodehouse was unable to deal with them save in a very general way.

X

The actual broadcasts

37.   The B.B.C. have furnished the Security Service with the information in their possession as to the number of broadcasts actually made and the audience to which they were directed. We do not know at present whether members of the Monitoring Staff of the B.B.C. will be in a position to prove actual reception of the broadcasts, but this matter will be enquired into.

I understand that only Talk No. 1 was fully recorded, either mechanically or in shorthand, by the B.B.C.; the remainder of the talks appear to have been summarised only. Prior to my arrival in Paris, Wodehouse had handed to Major M. Muggeridge of the Intelligence Corps the "script" of the five talks which he recorded. When I was interviewing Wodehouse I produced these to him and he told me that they were true versions of what he had actually recorded. Copies of these accompany this report, and I am satisfied that they correspond with the material in the possession of the B.B.C.

38. According to the B.B.C., Wodehouse's talks were broadcast as follows:

Date of talk	Audience to which addressed	Title
27.6.41	C.B.S. network from Berlin to America	Interview with Harry Flannery
28.6.41	In English to America	Talk 1. "First Instalment of Adventures"
1.7.41	To Far East	Repeat of Talk 1
2.7.41	To America	Repeat of Talk 1
9.7.41	To America	Talk 2. "Life in a French Prison"
23.7.41	To America	Talk 3. "Trials of a Travelling Internee"
30.7.41	To America	Talk 4. Self Justification and "Fourth Instalment of Adventures as Internee"
6.8.41	To America	Talk 5. "Life in an Internment Camp in Silesia"
9.8.41	To England	Talk 1
10.8.41	To England	Talk 2
11.8.41	To England	Talk 3
12.8.41	To England	Talk 4
14.8.41	To England	Talk 5

39. The B.B.C. inform us that on July 30th, prior to the broadcasting of
Talk 4 to America, Wodehouse made the following remarks:

"Before I begin the fourth of a series of five broadcasts dealing with my
internment in Germany I should like to say a few words on another subject.
The Press and public of England seem to have jumped to the conclusion
that I have been in some way bribed or intimidated into making these
broadcasts. This is not the case. I did not make a bargain, as they put it, and
buy my release by agreeing to speak over the radio. I was released because I
am sixty years old or shall be in October. The fact that I was freed a few
months before that date was due entirely to the efforts of my friends, people
like (Devered?) Best [sic] of the Saturday Evening Post. As I pointed out in
my second talk, if I had been sixty when I was interned I should have been
released at the end of the first week.

"My reason for broadcasting is a simple one. In the course of my period of internment I received hundreds of letters of sympathy from American readers of my books who are strangers to me and I was naturally anxious to let them know how I had got on. Under existing conditions it was impossible to answer these letters but I did not want to be so ungrateful and ungracious as to seem to be ignoring them and the radio suggested itself as a solution . . .''

40.   On August 9th, prior to the broadcasting of Talk 1 to England, Wodehouse, according to the B.B.C., again made introductory remarks as follows:
"The five talks which follow are word for word as they were given over the radio by me to the United States. They were designed simply as a way of acknowledging the hundreds of sympathetic letters which I received during my internment from American readers of my books – letters which I have no other means of answering. They have caused violent attacks on me in England, but I still cannot see that there is anything in them which could not have been printed in any English newspaper and which would not have been so printed if I had been in a position to write for English newspapers. It never occurred to me that there could be anything harmful in such statements as that when in camp I read Shakespeare, that the Commandant at Huy Citadel had short legs and did not like walking uphill, that men who had no tobacco smoked tea and that there was an unpleasant smell in my cell at Loos Prison."
After the outcry against Wodehouse in England references were made to the controversy over the German radio on July 23rd and on November 19th 1941 by one E. D. Ward @ Edward Leo Delaney, an Irish American who was broadcasting for the enemy. It is unnecessary to set out Delaney's remarks here.

XI

The effect of Wodehouse's broadcasts on public opinion in England

41.   It appears that it was on June 25th, 1941, that an Associated Press message was received in London from Berlin indicating that Nazi officials had stated that Wodehouse had been released from internment. The Stockholm Correspondent of "The Times" in a message which appeared in that paper on June 27th, and which was dated June 26th, reported that Wodehouse had been interviewed by the Berlin Correspondent of the Swedish paper, "Aftonbladet", at the Hotel Adlon. Below this report appeared a British United Press message stating that Wodehouse was going to broadcast to the United States once a week on his experiences. The public reaction was immediate and highly critical. On July 3rd letters criticising Wodehouse from A. A. Milne and E. C. Bentley appeared in "The Daily

Telegraph", and hostile references to Wodehouse, both by way of letters to the Press and Press comment, continued well into August. The Southport Town Council, for example, resolved that all books by Wodehouse should be withdrawn from their libraries. On July 15th there took place a B.B.C. broadcast by "Cassandra", the "Daily Mirror" columnist. This was a very strong attack indeed on Wodehouse, and was itself the cause of some controversy as some people wrote to the Press suggesting that Wodehouse was being too severely condemned.

42.   Press references to Wodehouse continued at intervals right up to September 1st, 1944, when he was interviewed by the "Daily Sketch" correspondent, J. D'Arcy Dawson, in Paris.

XII

Wodehouse's apologia

43.   I have already drawn attention to the explanations made by Wodehouse in July and August 1941 over the radio.

In his statement to me Wodehouse used this phrase "now that I have explained how the broadcasts actually came to take place, I should like to deal with my motives in making them. In the first place, I was feeling intensely happy in a mood that demanded expression and, at the same time, I was very grateful to all my American friends and very desirous of doing something to return their kindness in sending me letters and parcels. There was also, I am afraid, a less creditable motive. I thought that people hearing the talks would admire me for having kept cheerful under difficult conditions, but I think I can say that what chiefly led me to make the talks was gratitude. I have thought this matter over very carefully and where the account which I have just given differs from that contained in my letter to the Foreign Office, I wish the former to be accepted. At the time when I wrote to the Foreign Office I was very worried."

Later he says, "I should like to conclude by saying that I never had any intention of assisting the enemy and that I have suffered a great deal of mental pain as a result of my action."

44.   In order to illustrate his frame of mind at the time of the broadcasts Wodehouse sets out in his statement his recollection of certain telegrams exchanged between the "Saturday Evening Post" in America and himself. The Editor of that journal was disturbed at the idea of Wodehouse broadcasting and, in the course of the telegrams, Wodehouse, so he says, tried to indicate that he could see no harm in giving the type of talk which had been arranged.

Wodehouse says that it was not until his wife arrived in Berlin towards the end of July that he realised, as a result of what she said to him, the effect which his talks had had in England. He says "I realised what a hideous mistake I had made and I have been longing for an opportunity ever since of putting myself right".

When interviewed by the "Daily Sketch" Correspondent in Paris Wodehouse described what had happened as "my terrible mistake".

45.   In June 1943 Wodehouse had sent a letter to the Foreign Office in which he gave an explanation of his actions, and on September 4th he addressed a letter to the Home Secretary from Paris, in which he said that he was most anxious to do everything possible "to clear it up".

XIII

The activities of Wodehouse in Germany after his broadcasts

46.   Prior to the arrival of his wife in Berlin towards the end of July 1941 Wodehouse, according to his statement, was handed 250 marks by Plack in payment for the broadcasts "which", he says, "I accepted, not realising the implications".

47.   Until the end of November 1941 the Wodehouses stayed with the Baroness von Bodenhausen in the Harz Mountains; they then returned to Berlin and were at the Adlon Hotel until April 1942; Wodehouse then went again to the home of the Baroness von Bodenhausen, but his wife remained in Berlin. In November 1942 Wodehouse returned to Berlin staying at the Adlon Hotel with his wife, save for one month which they spent at the Bristol Hotel. In April 1943 they went as paying guests to the Count and Countess Wolkenstein of Lobris, Upper Silesia. In September 1943, with the approach of winter, it appears that Mrs. Wodehouse was frightened of the air-raids on Berlin and that Dr. Schmidt was therefore approached for permission to spend the winter in Paris. This was granted.

During the time that Wodehouse was in Germany he continued his literary work. He states that two novels and two short stories were taken to America by Mr. Robert Chalker of the American Embassy in Berlin upon the latter's return to the United States in April 1942.

48.   It will be necessary to make enquiries in Germany in due course as to the conduct of the Wodehouses while they were in that country after the broadcasts. I fear that we shall find that their behaviour has been unwise. From what I have seen of Mrs. Wodehouse I expect to learn that she conducted herself in a flamboyant manner and that she accepted all the attention which was no doubt paid to her by German officials. Apart of course from the unwisdom of such conduct, if it took place, the basic matter

with which we are concerned is not affected. Indeed, it seems that Mrs Wodehouse was escorted from France to Germany by a Foreign Office official and that a good deal of fuss was made of her during the journey and upon her arrival in Berlin. She has, if anything, less political sense than her husband and I fear that she would not know how to conduct herself in the circumstances which arose. She did, however, realise quite clearly the harm that the broadcasts had done to Wodehouse.

49.   At some stage during their stay in Germany the Wodehouses did make efforts to obtain repatriation, about which they were not clear, but these will have to be the subject of further enquiry as they were unable to provide me with any details. The German Foreign Office records and those of the United States and Swiss Governments should provide information on this point.

XIV

The activities of Wodehouse in Paris

50.   The Wodehouses were escorted from Berlin to Paris by some official of the German Foreign Office. Werner Plack, when in Paris, used to stay at the Hotel Bristol and it appears that he recommended this hotel to the Wodehouses. The life of the Wodehouses in the Hotel Bristol is dealt with in a statement made by M. Marcel Vidal, the manager of that hotel. A statement has also been taken from M. A. L. Ipsen, a Danish citizen residing in Paris, and a letter was addressed to me by M. G. Elm, a Swedish journalist. These two gentlemen were mentioned to me by the Wodehouses as persons whom they would like to have interviewed about their conduct in Paris.
    Though the information thus obtained is favourable to the Wodehouses, I shall not be surprised if we receive complaints as to their conduct while in Paris and these will, of course, be investigated. Such complaints will no doubt arise from the attention paid to them by German officers and officials. I think that Wodehouse may have been in rather a difficult position in this regard because it was not easy for him to ignore a German who might choose to speak to him, and that same applies, perhaps to a greater degree, to Mrs. Wodehouse. The Intelligence staff in Paris will of course report any information on this subject which may be conveyed to them.
    Steps will, of course, be taken in Paris, as opportunity may offer, to see whether there is any evidence of any more serious act of collaboration with the enemy on the part of Wodehouse or his wife.

51.   I visited the Prefecture of Police but they had no record relating to the conduct of the Wodehouses in Paris, and it appears that the Prefecture was not officially notified by the Germans of their arrival in that city. Wode-

house told me that he had to report once a week at the Gestapo Headquar ters in the Rue des Saussaies, which was located in a building used in normal times as the Headquarters of the Sûreté Nationale. Major Mugger-idge of the Intelligence Corps has been in touch with the French Military Security Service in order to find out whether any documents relating to the Wodehouses had been found at Gestapo Headquarters, but I understand that up to the present this is not the case. The Gestapo destroyed their records before leaving. This matter will be kept in mind but I doubt if any records will be found.

XV

The finances of Wodehouse while in Germany and France

52. Wodehouse prepared a financial statement which he handed to me and this is attached to this report. As appears from the additional statement made by Wodehouse, he now has some doubt as to whether the account of expenditure given therein is accurate. Mrs. Wodehouse gives additional information as to their finances and we are provided with material which can be investigated in due course in Germany.

So far as concerns the loans, mentioned in the statement as having been made in Paris by Count Sollohub and Mr. Rotge, the picture dealer, I have satisfied myself by interviewing these two persons that the loans attributed to them were in fact made. Both of them found it convenient to advance money in this way, as it is to their advantage to have a creditor who may ultimately repay them in London or New York.

53. After having completed his first statement, Wodehouse addressed a letter to me in which he deals with the sale by him in 1942 of certain film rights to the Berliner Film Company for a sum of 40,000 marks. He asked me if this was an offence against the Trading with the Enemy regulations, but I told him I was unable to advise him on this matter. In the same letter he describes how he sold a novel to Messrs. Tauchnitz.

In an additional statement made by Mrs. Wodehouse she describes how, during the time when I was actually in Paris, she received a sum of 560,000 Francs from the Swiss Consulate General, this being money which had been remitted to her from Germany. She is unable to say how this sum is made up, and I have asked the British Embassy in Paris to request detailed information on this subject from the Swiss Consulate General.

54. Though the financial position of the Wodehouses is far from clear, it is plain that by the sale of film rights and of a novel in Germany, by the sale of jewelry [sic] and by borrowing, they acquired suf-ficient money to enable them to live comfortably. Wodehouse says in his statement that, apart

from the 250 marks handed to him by Plack in payment for the five broadcasts, he has never received financial assistance in any form from the German authorities either directly or indirectly.

XVI

Observations

55.   In my opinion it will not be possible to arrive at a final conclusion on this case until the various enquiries which I have indicated are made in Germany.

56.   It seems clear that the actual text of the Wodehouse broadcasts does not contain material of a pro-German character, and the view may well be taken that the mere words used by Wodehouse in his broadcasts were unlikely to assist the enemy.

Upon the information at present available it seems, subject always to the decision of the Director of Public Prosecutions, that Wodehouse has not been guilty of treasonable conduct and that his conduct does not bring him within the terms of Section 1 of the Treachery Act 1940.

It may, however, be considered that by lending his voice and his personality to the German broadcasting station, Wodehouse did an act which was likely to ass-ist the enemy. Did he do so "with intent to assist the enemy?" He claims that he had no such intention. On the other hand, it seems clear that the normal and probable consequence of his act in lending his voice to the enemy must have been to assist the enemy.

The question therefore arises as to whether or not Wodehouse has offended against Regulation 2A of the Defence (General) Regulations 1939, that is to say, has he, with intent to assist the enemy, done an act which is likely to assist the enemy?

If, of course, enquiries in Germany show that Wodehouse obtained his release upon condition that he should broadcast, the intention to assist the enemy will become plain indeed. If, on the other hand, the account given by Wodehouse in his statement is confirmed, it may be that a jury would find difficulty in convicting him of an intention to assist the enemy.

It is appreciated that the question of prosecuting Wodehouse raises matters of policy in addition to, and apart from, the questions of law involved.

I suggest, therefore, that a copy of this report and the accompanying documents should be placed before the Director of Public Prosecutions at this stage so that he may have an early opportunity of considering the issues raised by the conduct of Wodehouse while abroad.

59. [sic] In the meantime Wodehouse and his wife are living at the Hotel

166

Bristol in Paris, and they have been instructed by me that they must on no account change their residence without permission. Major Malcolm Muggeridge of the Intelligence Corps, who is in Paris, is keeping in constant touch with them. The British Embassy are aware of their presence in Paris, as are S.H.A.E.F., and both have been requested not to grant them permission to return to the United Kingdom without reference to the Home Office and the Security Service.

In the event of conditions in Paris rendering it undesirable for them to remain in that city, Major Muggeridge will make such arrangements for their residence elsewhere in France as appear expedient. There is a possibility, though I hope it will not occur, of French people giving expression to their disapproval of the conduct of the Wodehouses and it is in the event of anything of this kind occurring that the possibility of their leaving their present hotel has been borne in mind. I have strongly advised Wodehouse to refrain from giving any more interviews to the Press, though it remains to be seen whether he is capable of carrying out this advice.

E. J. P. Cussen, Major
M.I.5
28.9.44

167